The Adult Baby – An Identity on the Dissociation Spectrum

By Dylan Lewis
with Dax Jordan

Dedication:

To my wife for her constant love and wisdom.

To Rosalie Bent and Michael Bent for letting adult babies (and the world) know we aren't mad, bad or alone.

Contents

The Adult Baby – An Identity on the Dissociation Spectrum

The Adult Baby – An Identity on the Dissociation Spectrum

Foreword

In 2011, Rosalie and I set out to write a book about Adult Babies.

Initially, we were unsure about exactly what to write and the scope of the topic. This was because the amount of non-fiction material available about ABs was appalling small and much of it was of little to no value. Being an adult baby and wearing nappies was considered just a sexual fetish and as someone who has wanted nappies since I was three years old, I knew that to be nonsense. So, we spent a lot of time researching and interviewing other adult babies and we fell upon a definition that we perhaps had known all along. Adult Babies are subjectively *real* babies and toddlers. It is not a sexual fetish but, it is is in fact, a viable *personal identity*. And so the book, *"There's still a baby in my bed!"* was born, not in small part out of personal pain and a desire to help others avoid or mitigate that pain.

We now understand a lot more and accept that the adult baby is a complex, almost incomprehensible person that is both adult and infant, often at the same time. The causes, the structure of this is only just now being slowly revealed. PhD candidates are now looking at the detail of AB life having finally – and long overdue – recognising that it is not a sexual fetish at all, but a genuine regressive identity that both needs – and demands – acceptance.

Our book was never intended to be the final word. Rather, we hoped that others would take up the mantle and continue the task of discovering more about who we are and how we can deal with it. Dylan Lewis is one of the foremost authors and researchers in this field and this latest book is his crowning achievement.

The notion of dissociation is a scary one. It certainly scared me, even though I suspected it to be true from my very early years. I am sure it scares you too, but this brilliantly-crafted book removes the fears and replaces it with facts, understanding and a comprehensive 'aha!' moment of finally putting the pieces into place.

The Adult Baby – An Identity on the Dissociation Spectrum

This book is *the* next step in understanding the complexities of the adult baby and opens windows that let light and fresh air into a soul that may be stale and listless because it stands alone and hidden. But we stand alone no longer because we know that who we are and who we can become, is both real and refreshingly healthy.

Dylan Lewis is to be applauded for taking his own experience of being an adult baby and enlightening us all about who we are.

It is okay to be an adult baby. And now we know why.

Michael and Rosalie Bent

1. Introduction

Being an adult baby is a big deal.

It is a mind-blowing, one-in-a-thousand identity.

I am an AB – an Adult Baby. At some point, each of us realizes our psyche is hard-wired differently to everyone else we know.

We are sane, functional adults. Yet we have a compelling need to wear nappies. They comfort something deep inside us. We need to see ourselves in nappies. We want others to see us wearing them (whether we act on that or not). Many of us at least wet them. Many of us fantasize about being babied – cuddled, changed, fed, disciplined etcetera. And that's without all the rest – stuffed toys, pacifiers, baby clothes, bottles etc.

WTF!

It is no wonder coming to terms with being an AB isn't simple.

This is a book for ABs who are ready to understand that nappies are the tip of the psychological iceberg. It is about understanding ourselves so that we can live happily and safely as ABs.

Accepting being AB is a permanent and central part of my psyche and sent me on a journey to understand exactly why that is true. I'm the kind of person who hates not knowing. I can (eventually) handle difficult truths, much better than I can handle not knowing.

I discovered being AB is an identity on the dissociation spectrum. That's the same spectrum as Dissociative Identity Disorder (DID) - which used to be known as Multiple Personality Disorder (MPD).

For some ABs, that information may be unwelcome. I can imagine the internal dialogues – "shit! It's tough enough already accepting or explaining being AB, and you go and dump being crazy on top!"

The Adult Baby – An Identity on the Dissociation Spectrum

Hear me out. Forget the movies. Dissociation does *not* equal crazy. There are many high-functioning people with some form of dissociation. It forms a broad spectrum. Everyone on the spectrum has an individual 'footprint' with its own unique experience of self and life. DID is at the further end of the spectrum, and being AB is akin to *next door*. Dissociation is common. It is estimated ten per cent of the population has substantial levels of dissociation. That makes it as common as mood disorders like depression and anxiety. As with ABs, people with dissociation do not disclose and commonly hide amongst us in plain sight.

I believe dissociation is the most valid way of explaining being AB. Let's face it, the hard wiring in our psyche is pretty different and rather deep. You know that because, like most ABs at some time or other, you have tried giving it up. Any valid explanation for being AB is going to have to go pretty deep into the psyche. There is no clear empirical or clinical evidence backing any explanation. We are left to make up our own minds based on our logic, reading and self-reflection. The other explanations for being AB are shallow ('it's a kink') or fall into the category of 'bad or mad' – it's a fetish or a psycho-sexual disorder. Dissociation not only offers a better explanation, it also shows how being AB can be a healthy and stable personal identity.

This book explores 'being AB' as an identity on the dissociation spectrum. It does that through a comparison between being AB and DID. You may be an AB who finds a comparison with DID confronting. That is understandable. I ask you to set aside preconceptions and prejudice about DID – the same way, as ABs, we ask others to set aside their preconceptions and prejudice about us.

TRIGGER WARNING: If you are in the initial stages of understanding your identity, either with DID or being AB, a comparison with another misunderstood minority identity may be over-loading and confronting. You may wish to put this book aside for a later time.

What is the benefit of the comparison? There is a compelling similarity between the two identities. Both have alternate personalities which powerfully shape their experience of self and

The Adult Baby – An Identity on the Dissociation Spectrum

life. For ABs, it is our child alters who need nappies and all the rest, to feel recognized, nurtured and safe. For both identities our reality is subjective. It is invisible and incomprehensible to others. There is no way of directly proving the existence of alternative personalities to a doubting person. They are visible only through behaviours which are otherwise inexplicably at odds with the personality we present to the world.

I liken being AB to finding out you are adopted. Adoptees are confronted by the fact they do not share DNA with those around them. That's like ABs realizing our psyches are hard-wired differently than everyone else's. For me, realizing I shared some of my hard-wiring with people with DID was like an adopted person finding their only close living relative. At last, someone who really gets what it's like to live with the subjective reality of an alter which is compelling to me, but incomprehensible to others. Someone who can help me understand the wiring in my psyche. Some people with DID refer to themselves as 'multiples'. ABs often refer to themselves as having a 'Little' and an adult side. We are multiples too – a different kind from people with DID – but still multiples.

The comparison is largely between one AB (myself, Dylan) and one person with DID – Dax, my co-author. Dax is a member of my extended family. He is high functioning, a teacher who taught special needs children around the world. I also read autobiographies, case histories and the published work of four psychiatrists who know DID. Each AB or person with DID is unique. No one individual can be representative, but I hope Dax and myself exemplify some of the key traits and issues for our respective identities.

The book shows what it feels like to live with DID and being AB – when it feels similar and when it feels different. There are compelling similarities between the child alters of ABs and people with DID. It also demonstrates being AB is not DID. There are clear differences. The comparison pinpoints what they are.

Why did I think of this comparison? Let me explain. Until my early fifties, I experienced being AB largely as a conflicted sexual fetish – nothing to do with identity, dissociation or DID. Then Dax visited from overseas and stayed with my wife and myself several times over two years. My wife is a psychotherapist. She suggested that like Dax, I too might have alternative personalities. The thought fell on fertile ground – a few years before I had read Rosalie Bent's ground-breaking book *'There's a Baby In My Bed: Living With the Adult Baby in Your Relationship'*. It viewed being AB as an identity, not a fetish. Therapy confirmed I had child alters. It was an epiphany that revolutionized my understanding of my AB identity. My need to wear nappies, wear baby clothes and all the rest, was not the product of a sexual fetish, but having a subjectively real alternative personality, a very young child.

That discovery caused me to change my view of dissociation. I could be 'messed up' at times, but I am a sane and functional adult. I have a long happy marriage and I am happily retired from a successful career. That didn't fit with the uninformed view of dissociation as crazy and debilitating.

Understanding that ABs are multiples also helps us understand our complicated sexuality. A later chapter shows the unconscious logic behind our sexual needs and compulsions.

This book is a collaboration between Dax and myself. I asked lots of questions about DID, and advanced hypotheses about the similarities and differences between the two identities. Dax sent me lengthy emails explaining his experience of DID and responding to my hypotheses. On this basis, I prepared the text which Dax reviewed. Dax's grasp on DID is insightful and articulate. I believe the most compelling understanding of DID comes where I have quoted directly from his emails.

This is a self-help book. The key audience is ABs and those who love them. It assumes you know a lot about ABs and where you fit on the ABDL spectrum, but know less about dissociation and DID. The book is my best attempt to understand our shared identity. I have no formal qualifications in psychology, but I have a layman's lifelong interest in the subject. Every AB is different, and some will disagree with my views. I do not intend to disparage those whose views are different from mine.

The Adult Baby – An Identity on the Dissociation Spectrum

As adults, we all construct our own identities, based on what we choose to believe about ourselves. Those beliefs can change over time and our identity changes with it. At any point in time, our identity represents what we need to believe to feel safe and okay, with ourselves. In terms of our personal identity, no one has the right to tell us what we should believe about ourselves. So, if after scanning or reading this book, you want to think of being AB as a kink, or a fetish, and/or being AB has nothing to do with subjectively real alters or childhood trauma, that's okay. That's you, defining you. This book is about offering people information based on my best honest understanding, and giving them a choice about what they believe. Take what is helpful from the book and leave the rest behind.

The other intended audience is mental health professionals, who I hope will be prompted to think more deeply about the AB identity. The health professions' present ways of understanding 'being AB' are just labels that explain little or nothing. How can the obvious pointers to fundamental issues in AB's early childhood be ignored? How can being AB be thought of as just a paraphilia or sexual fetish? Sure, it is often a fetish as part of its expression. That's a symptom, not the cause. It doesn't explain why ABs seek and derive emotional comfort from their nappies and fantasies of infancy. How long can the involuntary character of many AB behaviours (triggering etc) - so at odds with the AB's adult personality - be viewed simply as a compulsion or addiction? These symptoms require dissociation and repressed childhood trauma be included in any competent differential diagnosis.

This book is based on the pioneering work of Rosalie Bent and Michael Bent in identifying and understanding ABs as a personal identity. I recommend their books and website *abdiscovery.com.au* . I refer to their insights throughout the book.

By adult baby, I exclude role players and diaper lovers for whom diapers, baby clothes or baby activities are an optional extra they can freely live without, and pure fetishists for whom these things are confined exclusively to sexual expression.

17

The Adult Baby – An Identity on the Dissociation Spectrum

This book follows my *'The Adult Baby Identity'* trilogy – *'Coming Out as an Adult Baby'*, *'Healing Childhood Wounds'*, and *'A Self Help Guide'*.

The journey of self-discovery is not an easy one to undertake alone. You need a confidant who you can trust, and who will be an ally in your healing. If there is no one in your life with whom you can safely share your feelings about your life as an adult baby, seek professional support – preferably from an LGBTQ-friendly therapist who understands dissociation and personal identity. If you are in crisis or deep distress about being an adult baby seek professional therapy.

2. Preview

There were times when researching this book was a revelation for me. I was very surprised to see the similarity between the child selves of AB's, their 'Littles', and the child alters of people with DID.

Below are two accounts of a 'Little' or child alter written by the person's partner. See if you can pick the one that belongs to an AB, and the one that belongs to a person with DID. I have edited out identifying text but otherwise, the accounts are quoted verbatim.

Account 1

[Chrissy's husband says] "Chrissy [was] so excited to be out and about with me, seeing all of these wonderful new sights. ... We had barely walked half a block when Chrissy yanks me into a charming shop with a variety of handmade wooden toys, puzzles and dolls. Chrissy is quietly sharing with me her delight and excitement of this wonderful world of toys. ... With much exuberance, she pulls me up the stairs to a wall loaded floor to ceiling with stuffed bears. ... Pink bears, green bears, and rainbow bears. The pleasure Chrissy feels in seeing the princess and ballerina bears light up her sparkling eyes. ... no one pays much attention until I push a button hidden in the first dancing bear's paw. The music starts and the graceful bear spins around and around. Before I can comprehend the implications of this one bear, Chrissy waltzes her way to five more paw-activated bears. Now they're all singing, laughing and talking while Chrissy cries out in joy and claps her hands. Soon even more of these once-cute but now loud and obnoxious bears are gyrating and convulsing, with Chrissy laughing all the way.

I soon feel that the situation is out of my control. I glance down the stairs and notice the shop owner scowling up at me. ... I don't want Chrissy to sense my discomfort. She is truly just experiencing what any child would the very first time in a toy store or even on Christmas Day. You wouldn't want to stifle a child then, but I am feeling anxious.

Sadly, I am unable to prevent Chrissy from noticing my discomfort, and what began as a splendid adventure of wonder turns into her feeling confused and ashamed. ... She sheds many tears while apologizing for embarrassing me. I hold her tight, trying to reassure her that she didn't embarrass me, the situation did."

Account 2

[Joanne's wife and mother says] "Joanne was happy and content and her needs were being well met. Then one overnight there was a storm. My little three-year-old is terrified of wind and storms at night and so we had night-time tears, fear and when morning came, there was just a scared little infant in bed and the adult was as far away as he has ever been. Joanne was thoroughly and irredeemable regressed and she would not and could not grow up. We had plans for that day. Adult plans. They were cancelled as there was no adult there – just an infant behaving at her youngest age level of 12 months old.

It was a difficult day. It was difficult to communicate with her beyond limited baby talk or gestures. By evening she was communicating better but the following morning there she was again, very little and quite regressed. I felt like we were still back in the nursery level.

It took two full days for her to really return back to her place of balance and peace and I am reminded again that just as in the parenting of physical children, you can do all the right things and still get bad things happen. Joanne is normally a delightful and happy child and it is an exciting and happy time for her and for me. But those two days were difficult for us both because for at least one of those days, we had lost control."

Account 1 is from Christine Pattillo's autobiography *'I Am We: My Life With Multiple Personalities'*, and is narrated by her husband who is the father of six-year-old alter Chrissy.

Account 2 is from Rosalie Bent's on-line blog (cited in the references). She is the wife of her AB husband, and mother to his 'Little', baby Joanne.

The Adult Baby – An Identity on the Dissociation Spectrum

You may have picked correctly, you may not. But I think the similarity in the character of the two accounts is compelling. The similarity is not a one-off. I chose these two out of a larger sample cited in Chapter 9. Compare Rosalie Bent's account with another description of a similar night-time incident by Christine Pattillo.

> "Well, last night there was a small windstorm in our neighbourhood ... We were all snoozing soundly when a power transformer, less than a mile away, shorted out. The sound was like a gunshot and startled Chrissy, even though she was asleep inside Cita's [Christine Pattillo] mind. Chrissy's fear was so acute she burst into tears and shifted right out, waking Christopher. Christopher immediately began to comfort her and calm her down."

The similarity represents the two closest points in the experience of DID and AB. Christine Pattillo's account of her DID is unusual in the warmth and openness with which she and her family have embraced her child alters. Rosalie Bent's husband is a regressive AB. The latter term is one used by Rosalie to describe ABs who have a powerful need to express their 'Little'.

Many people with these two identities would not have this degree of commonality in their experience and expression of self. But even where the overlap is not so strong, I believe it is still there. The rest of this book is about exploring the origin and nature of that commonality.

Rosalie and Michael Bent are the foremost public authorities on the adult baby identity. Rosalie is the wife of Michael, an adult baby. In 2012 Rosalie published the landmark book 'There's A Baby in My Bed' intended for the partners of adult babies. It was the first published work to seriously address adult babies as a personal identity, beyond a sexual fetish. It was updated in 2015 as 'There's Still A Baby in My Bed. Rosalie has also written a book for the parents of teenage adult babies. Michael has published a text 'Adult Babies: Psychology and Practices' and an anthology of insightful articles 'Being An Adult Baby'. Rosalie and Michael are the owners of the

The Adult Baby – An Identity on the Dissociation Spectrum
website abdiscovery.com.au which is dedicated to helping adult babies understand themselves, and fostering public understanding of the identity.

3. Dissociation

I believe dissociation is key to understanding ABs.

To help guide an understanding of dissociation, this book references the published writing of four psychiatrists.

Marlene Steinberg is an American who developed a key diagnostic questionnaire for dissociative conditions, the *Structured Clinical Interview for Clinical Disorders* (SCID-D), sometimes cited as the gold standard for such identification. Her excellent 2010 book *'The Stranger in the Mirror: the Hidden Epidemic'* demystifies dissociation and DID. Contrary to the prevailing wisdom she focused on dissociation from the beginning of her career in the early 1990s.

David Yeung is a Canadian who retired in 2006 after a forty-year career. He worked with about one hundred DID clients in the latter half of his career. He was concerned at the scarcity of mental health professionals willing and able to work with DID clients. After retirement, he wrote a set of case studies and therapeutic guidelines for mental health professionals (*'Engaging Multiple Personalities' Volumes 1 and 2*). His approach is notably empathic and client-centred.

Colin A. Ross (b. 1950) is another Canadian. He is a widely published authority on trauma and dissociation, and the author of a key textbook on DID, *'Dissociative Identity Disorder: Diagnosis, Clinical Features, and Treatment of Multiple Personality'*. He developed another key diagnostic questionnaire for dissociative disorders, the *Dissociative Disorders Interview Schedule* (DDIS). His grounded approach emphasizes working with the internal logic of DID. He has powerful insight but understates the subjective reality of alters. I draw most on his recent (2018) book *'Treatment of Dissociative Identity Disorder: Techniques and Strategies for Stabilisation'*.

Jeffrey Smith is an American. He was the therapist of Robert Oxnam, one of the most high-profile people who have 'come out' with DID. The latter is known for his 2013 autobiography *'A*

Fractured Mind: My Life With Multiple Personality Disorder'. Dr Smith does not claim to be an authority on DID/MPD. However, his epilogue to the above autobiography, *'Understanding DID Therapy: The Case of Robert B. Oxnam by Jeffrey Smith MD'*, is outstanding for its insight and clarity.

What is Dissociation?

In essence, dissociation means detachment or disconnection - detachment from external factors (others, the environment), or detachment from the self, or both. Dr Colin Ross states –

> *"Dissociation basically means disconnection. A person can be disconnected from thoughts, feelings, memories, sensations or any aspect of the mind and body."*

Dissociation is a common and functional coping mechanism for dealing with a range of situations. It can be voluntary, such as when there is a compelling need for intense single-minded focus, or involuntary, such as in a car accident or a heart attack.

Dr Yeung gives an example of a common, functional example of dissociation –

> *"Dissociation is not always pathological. For example, a surgeon in the midst of a nasty divorce must remain able to concentrate in the operating room. The act of separating the ordinary stream of divorce-related thoughts from the task of surgery at hand requires effective dissociation."* [Engaging Multiple Personalities (Volume 1): Contextual Case Histories.]

Colin Ross comments:

> *"... every woman who has given birth has been in an extreme dissociative state."*

In sudden trauma, dissociation involuntarily quarantines incapacitating fear or pain in one part of the psyche so we can

continue to function. Dr Steinberg defines traumatic dissociation as
-

> *"...an adaptive defence in response to high stress or trauma characterized by memory loss and a sense of disconnection from oneself or one's surroundings". ... To help us survive, certain perceptions, feelings, sensations, thoughts, and memories related to the trauma are split off from full awareness and encoded in some peripheral level of awareness. Miraculously, dissociation alters reality, but allows the person to stay in contact with it in order to help himself." [The Stranger in the Mirror: Dissociation The Hidden Epidemic]*

There are many misconceptions about dissociation. I discovered it –

1. is a broad spectrum ranging from mild forms through to clinical conditions;
2. is a lot more common than people think;
3. need not prevent a person from being functional and successful;
4. has five components which may be present in differing combinations and strengths depending on the individual, so everyone with dissociation has their own unique 'footprint'.

Let's look at each of these.

Spectrum

The spectrum ranges from -

- mild dissociation which can take such forms as an intense single-minded focus, or 'zoning out' from disturbing or confronting situations;
- sub-clinical dissociation which involves altered states of consciousness, which may have a significant effect on a person's experience of self and life, but does not trigger medical intervention; and

- clinical conditions which trigger medical intervention and include separate streams of consciousness, identity and/or self. These can include a sense the self or the world is unreal (depersonalization and derealization), fragmentation of identity, such as DID, or complex post-traumatic stress disorder.

More Common Than You Think

The Wikipedia article 'Dissociation (psychology) states –

"... in the normal population, dissociative experiences that are not clinically significant are highly prevalent with 60% to 65% of the respondents indicating that they have had some dissociative experiences."

A recent meta-analysis of around one hundred other studies indicated around 10 per cent of the population would meet the criteria for a dissociative disorder (see *'The prevalence of Dissociative Disorders and dissociative experiences in college'* by Mary-Anne Kate in the references). Dr Steinberg's 2010 book cites a survey which estimates that 14 per cent of the US population experiences *substantial* dissociative symptoms. These figures indicate the prevalence of dissociative conditions is on a par with the better known and accepted mood disorders such as depression and anxiety.

DID, the most extreme form of dissociation, used to be thought of as very rare. That's no longer thought to be true. Within the broader population with substantial dissociation symptoms, Dr Steinberg estimates up to one per cent of the population may have DID. Wikipedia, in the article on DID, cites a figure of two per cent. The International Society for the Study of Trauma and Dissociation's (ISSTD) 2010 Guidelines for Treating Dissociative Identity Disorder in Adults cite estimates that one to three per cent of the population have DID.

The Adult Baby – An Identity on the Dissociation Spectrum

Doesn't Stop People Being Successful

There are many high functioning people with dissociative conditions. Dr Steinberg states that they –

"... run the gamut from PhDs to prostitutes and are generally highly intelligent, creative, brave, articulate and likeable. Many are accomplished professionals, married, raising children, holding down responsible jobs."

People with DID work successfully in many walks of life. Dr Yeung states –

"Without conscious effort, many DID persons utilize their dissociative abilities to enhance their work. Teachers with DID can be exceptionally perceptive and sensitive to their students' difficulties because their young alters easily attune to their students' needs. Similarly, a therapist with alters can be readily attuned to their patients in therapeutic work."

Amongst the autobiographies of people with DID I read, one person was a high powered US Department of Justice lawyer (Olga Trujillo), another a prominent international academic (Robert Oxam), and another a very high profile sportsperson in the US NFL (Herschel Walker).

Because of fear of being thought crazy people with dissociative conditions commonly do not disclose. Friends, colleagues and acquaintances are mostly not aware the person has a dissociative condition. Given the prevalence indicated above, it is very likely one or more of the people you interact with on a weekly basis have, or have had, substantial dissociative symptoms (in the same way you interact with people who have depression or anxiety).

Components

Dr Steinberg identifies five components of dissociation. These are -

1. Amnesia – gaps in memory or 'lost time';

2. Depersonalisation – a feeling of detachment from your emotions or your body, or looking at yourself as an outsider would;
3. Derealization – a feeling of detachment from your environment, such as feeling the environment or other people aren't real, or familiar people are Strangers;
4. Identity confusion – a feeling of uncertainty, puzzlement or conflict about who you are - perhaps a continuing struggle going on inside you to define yourself; and
5. Identity alteration – a shift in role or identity, accompanied by such changes in your behaviour that are observable to others – you may experience the shift as a personality switch or loss of control over yourself to someone else inside you.

Each individual on the dissociation spectrum has a different 'footprint'. They may have all five components or only some, and in different strengths. Each different 'footprint' produces a unique experience of self and life. Your footprint is *your* footprint. Accepting that you are on the dissociation spectrum doesn't mean your experience has to conform to anyone else's.

Identity Alteration

It is the fifth component - *identity alteration* - which is most important to understanding DID and being AB. People with identity alteration have one or more subjectively real personas, distinct from the host-birth personality. The depth of those personas can vary. With moderate levels of identity alteration, the personas maybe only two dimensional, feeling states – barely personas. With stronger levels of identity alteration, the personas have a repertoire of thoughts, emotions, capabilities, and needs that represent a fully formed alternative personality.

Dr Steinberg states -

The Adult Baby – An Identity on the Dissociation Spectrum

" ... research has found that identity alteration, as with all the dissociative symptoms, occurs along a spectrum of intensity: mild levels in the general population; mild to moderate levels in people with nondissociative psychiatric disorders, but also with people with dissociative disorder not otherwise specified (DDNOS); severe levels of identity alteration in people with dissociative identity disorder (DID).

A person with moderate levels of identity alteration may act as if he or she is like two (or more) different people, but it's not clear whether these identity alterations assume complete control of a person's behaviour or represent separate personalities. ...

Severe identity alteration, the *sina qua non* of DID, involves a person's shifting between distinct personality states that take control of his or her behaviour and thought. These alter personalities are more clearly defined and distinctive than the personality fragments that characterize moderate levels of identity alteration. Each alter has its own name, memories, traits and behaviour patterns.

Identity alteration differs from identity confusion in that identity confusion represents the internal dimension of identity disturbance, whereas identity alteration represents the external dimension. A person with identity confusion, in other words, has thoughts and feelings of uncertainty and conflict related to his or her identity; a person with identity alteration manifests the uncertainty and conflict **behaviourally**.

Trauma and Splitting

Alternative personalities emerged as the psyche's response to trauma, typically in early childhood. To understand that phenomena we need to recognize trauma can have deep and lasting effects on the psyche.

Dr Ross describes the nature of trauma –

"The impacts of trauma on a person can be profound, and multiple. Trauma could affect a person in terms of the

cognitive, behavioural, emotional, interpersonal and even physiological aspects of self. Why?

Trauma may make a person feel like the world is dangerous and unpredictable.

Trauma may make a person think that no one can be trusted.

Trauma may make a person believe that he/she is not loveable.

Trauma may make a person feel very angry, depressed or frightened.

Trauma may make a person try hard to avoid any similar situations and anything that could remind him/her of the traumatic event.

Trauma could profoundly affect one's body (eg. Amygdala, hippocampus, autonomic nervous system). After trauma, a person may become very sensitive and hyperaroused; his or her stress response systems are also affected, and he/she may have difficulty in relaxing or getting to sleep.

Trauma leaves a person with unprocessed memories and unaddressed emotions, which may become nightmares or lead to flashbacks." [Be a Teammate with Yourself: Understanding Trauma and Dissociation]

Trauma is a challenge for someone at any age. But it is particularly challenging for a child who's psyche is still dependent on the care and support of others. Trauma can be caused by abuse. It can also be caused by more mundane events - the 'ordinary catastrophes' of childhood such as accidents, temporary separations from caregivers, or bullying. It can happen in any situation where a child experiences great distress or fear, and feels themselves to be physically alone, or feels unprotected by those to whom they might look to for protection.

The Adult Baby – An Identity on the Dissociation Spectrum

In the face of overwhelming fear and distress, a child's psyche may 'split off' a distinct alter. This is a sub-conscious process. Dr Steinberg indicates the younger the child, the more susceptible they are to 'splitting'.

Dr Jeffrey Smith describes the process of traumatic 'splitting' -

Multiple personality begins with dissociation. When we note that adult victims of disaster seem to be in 'a daze', we are referring to dissociation. There is the dissociation of feeling from fact. Trauma survivors will often remember the moment they dissociated. For example, a child who was molested, focused on a spot on the ceiling. Soon she began to experience herself looking down dispassionately from the ceiling as if the girl below were someone else.

Where there is complete amnesia, the dissociation is more extensive, involving memory as well as feeling. ... what makes a particular trauma severe enough to trigger loss of memory? The first and foremost factor, in my view, is aloneness, the lack of a safe person to share the event. The need for human connection, especially in times of stress, begins very early in life. A six-year-old girl in the process of being abused by her drunken step-father was able to keep from being overwhelmed by hoping that her mother would soon return. When her mother did come back, the girl quickly realized that her mother was no more able to stand up to her abuser than she was. Suddenly aware that her hope was illusory ... she ran out of the house into the night. Years later, the only thing she remembered was the image of headlights shining in her eyes. Aloneness makes traumatic events much more damaging, and dissociation much more likely. [A Fractured Mind: My Life With Multiple Personality Disorder – Epilogue]

Splitting quarantines incapacitating fear and pain so the rest of the psyche can continue to function. It can also preserve attributes or capabilities that might otherwise be damaged or lost due to the trauma. Dr Smith states –

The Adult Baby – An Identity on the Dissociation Spectrum

"... when events overwhelm emotional defences, the damage is less when it can be encapsulated in dissociation. Trauma survivors who are not able to dissociate often sustain greater damage than those who are able to split. The harm to self-esteem and to the sense of safety affects their entire being. By contrast, multiples often have parts that are entirely spared the effects of trauma. There may be joyful, innocent children existing side by side with those personalities that have been most damaged."

Dr Yeung describes this response to trauma as the psyche's 'self-triage'. Splitting can occur multiple times as dissociation becomes the pattern for responses to trauma.

Repression and Denial

In cases of traumatic dissociation in adults, the memory of the traumatic event is commonly either never lost, or returns shortly afterwards. Dissociation linked to childhood trauma is different. It often has lasting effects on the psyche, effects which persist into adulthood. Yet despite those effects, the memory or full experience of the trauma may be hidden in the unconscious for many years and decades.

Both the original trauma and the resulting alter are initially buried in the sub-conscious in what is called repression. When the alter and memories are repressed we genuinely don't know they are there. It is amnesia.

Repression is key to understanding dissociation.

Based on my personal experience, I think of repression as a high wall. It was erected quickly in an emergency. It was not so much built, as 'thrown up', using whatever materials and labour were at hand. In places, the wall is made of big concrete blocks, well-mortared and on deep foundations, and will never come down. In other places, the wall is just house bricks, sometimes poorly mortared and without a solid footing beneath. In those places, the mortar ages and crumbles and eventually the bricks tumble down, leaving gaps in the wall.

The memories of trauma, and trauma-related experiences, such as the splitting of alters, are not only buried in the unconscious, they are stored in a way that makes their retrieval complex and uncertain. They are not stored as useable, accessible memories (explicit memory). Dr Smith explains the difference between explicit and implicit memory -

> *"Explicit memory is processed for storage in a structure [in the brain] known as the hippocampus, while implicit memory is more diffusely spread out in the brain. Simply stated, **explicit** refers to that which is in the foreground of our consciousness and accessible to language, while **implicit** refers to the background, or context, and is nonverbal."*

Dr Steinberg indicates that –

> *"the amygdala shapes and stores traumatic memories in the limbic part of the brain, which processes emotions and sensations, but not language or speech. As a result, survivors of childhood abuse may carry implicit physiological memories of the terror, pain, and sadness generated by the abuse but may have few or no explicit factual memories to explain their flashbacks and the feelings and sensations they arouse. They live with the repercussions of the event without having a narrative – this is what happened at this time or place – to provide a back story. Memories of traumatic experiences are not retrieved so much as they intrude. They pop up in jagged impressionistic fragments overloaded with sensations and emotions that can distort the details."*

This pattern of memory is applicable to any repressed trauma, not just abuse.

Over time repression breaks down - fragments of memory return. The buried, split off alter 'breaks through' and influences a person's thoughts, feelings, perceptions and behaviours, even when the source of that influence is unrecognized. Repression can start breaking down early. For example, ABs commonly start acting on their desire for nappies around age ten, or sometimes even earlier. That desire is compelling, but incomprehensible because it represents the first breakthrough of repressed unconscious needs.

After that has been happening for a while, repression can start to shade into denial. Unlike repression, denial is a product of the conscious mind. Therapist Lyn Mary Karjala explains -

> *"It [denial] happens when there's some aspect of the external world that's simply too painful for us to face, so we can't allow ourselves to see it. The classic example is the alcoholic who admits that he drinks but vehemently denies that he has a drinking problem, in spite of the mounting evidence that's increasingly apparent to people around him. He's not knowingly lying when he says he doesn't have a problem – he's genuinely unaware of it. In other words, he's kept the knowledge of his behaviour in his conscious awareness – he knows that he drinks – but he's dissociated the significance and the danger of the behaviour." ['Understanding Trauma and Dissociation: A Guide for Patients and Loved Ones']*

For this book, the reader might replace the reference to an alcoholic and drinking with an AB and their compulsive need for nappies. We might imagine hearing an AB say, *"its just a kink or fetish, nothing to do with deep issues in my psyche and my childhood ..."*

Dr Steinberg states –

> *" ... people suffering from a dissociative disorder often have a huge amount of denial. ... Their worst fear is that if they talk about their symptoms to a therapist, they'll immediately be labelled as a freak or a crazy person.*
>
> *Very often, people who have separate parts of themselves keep them hidden, because they don't think of them as well-defined personalities, but more as 'aspects' of their own personalities or different internal voices or puzzling 'sides' of themselves with which they are not in touch with all the time."*

The Adult Baby – An Identity on the Dissociation Spectrum
"One of the trickier aspects of dissociation is that the more chronic some symptoms are, the less stress they may cause because you've adapted to them and they have become as normal to you as breathing."

As a result of repression and then denial, it can take decades for the unconscious to release its' secrets. I mean decades! To change analogies, the way repression releases its grip on memory is like the front of a glacier where it meets the sea. Mostly it just melts, releasing the meltwater so slowly that it's imperceptible. But at other times, great blocks of ice will crack and fall off the glacier and crash into the sea throwing up a shower of spray. Then we will have blocks of memory suddenly return. Even years after self-acceptance and therapy, the unconscious continues to release new insights and memories.

Only those who have lived long enough to see the unconscious repression in their own early life break down and be revealed, understand its power. Trying to explain that to others, especially those in the first half of life, can be a bit like trying to explain colour to the colour-blind. Recognizing the power your unconscious has had over your life is confronting. It humbles our pride that we are the ones in conscious control. The first decades of adolescence and adulthood are about establishing that control. It is not a time of life well suited to recognize some of that hard-won control is illusory.

Dissociation Becomes Dysfunctional

We have seen that dissociation is functional when a child is faced with overwhelming trauma. It quarantines fear, hurt or pain within one part of the child's psyche so they can continue to function after the trauma. It protects resilience. Dissociation is a creative, subjective denial of objective reality.

However, continued reliance on dissociation when we are adolescents and adults can become dysfunctional. Denying objective reality becomes a two-edged sword. Some denial might not cause too much harm. But denying objective reality too much, or the parts of it that we need to heed to be safe and functional becomes dysfunctional and harmful. It reduces our resilience and makes us more psychologically vulnerable. That is what happens for people with severe uncontrolled DID.

If you have dissociated trauma in your childhood, the problem is that you don't pick and choose rationally when to use dissociative coping strategies as an adult. Those choices are being made in your sub-conscious and driven by the unhealed childhood trauma. And coming from that fearful and hurt place some of the choices will be bad ones. That's why it's important to identify and heal childhood trauma. Only that allows a person to make conscious and rational choices about how they cope with the difficulties they encounter.

The Dissociation Spectrum Revisited

Now that we are armed with a greater understanding of dissociation we can revisit the dissociation spectrum with greater precision. Dr Ross states –

> *"The spectrum of dissociation is often portrayed as: no symptoms at the left-hand end – symptoms but no diagnosable disorder – dissociative amnesia – depersonalization/derealization disorder – other specified dissociative disorder (OSDD) – DID at the right-hand end."* [Treatment of Dissociative Identity Disorder: Techniques and Strategies for Stabilisation"]

ABs who are confronted by the idea they are on the dissociation spectrum might find it easier to think of it as an 'inner child spectrum'. Dr Ross continues -

> *"... a good conceptual framework for the spectrum of dissociation is the inner child spectrum. The inner child is therapeutic lingo for unresolved feelings from childhood. The only question is: are these just feelings, or are they contained in an inner structure that has some degree of separateness from the adult self?*

The Adult Baby – An Identity on the Dissociation Spectrum

The inner child spectrum goes: no inner child – a metaphorical inner child – a sense of an inner child – a definite knowledge that there is an inner child inside – the inner child is visualized internally – the person and hear and talks to the inner child (DID)."

For ABs, the inner child is at the DID end of the spectrum. We may not hear the voice of the child in our heads, but their infantile needs result in persistent behaviours like wearing nappies, using pacifiers and baby clothing.

Summary

Dissociation means detachment from the self, or from the external environment, or both. Dissociation falls on a broad spectrum, ranging from common every-day, voluntary mental states through to involuntary, clinical conditions. Dissociation has five components. Every person on the dissociation spectrum has a different footprint, a unique combination of some or all of the five components, and in differing strengths. Each individual dissociation footprint produces a unique view of self and life.

Identity alteration, having distinct personalities or alters within the psyche, is one of the five components of dissociation. It comes from childhood trauma, where in response to overwhelming fear or pain, the psyche splits off an alter. That alter serves to quarantine the fear or pain to allow the rest of the psyche to function. It can also preserve attributes and capabilities within the psyche which would otherwise be damaged or lost. The memory of traumatic childhood dissociation is buried in the unconscious is what is called repression.

4. Dissociative Identity Disorder (DID) and being an Adult Baby (AB)

This chapter looks at DID and being AB and their respective places on the dissociation spectrum.

Concepts

To understand people with alternative personalities we need to use some concepts from DID.

A person who has an undivided, unitary psyche is called a 'singleton'. Anyone who has at least one alternative personality is called a 'multiple'. I use the term psyche to describe the whole person, whether a singleton or a multiple. When I use the term psyche for a multiple, it refers to all their parts (people with DID often use the term 'the system'). The 'host' is the personality who is out front most of the time. The host may, or may not be, the original personality from whom all the others sprang, directly or indirectly – the latter is the 'birth personality'. Each personality is called an 'alter', short for alternative personality (people with DID sometimes use the term 'parts').

For people with DID who's psyche is fragmented by amnesia, the total stock of memory is compartmentalized within different personalities. If fragmentation is reduced and personalities share memories, they are 'co-conscious'. A personality may be co-conscious with one or more other personalities, but not necessarily all.

The personality who is in executive control of the person's body is 'out', and others are 'in' (meaning inside). When the personality in executive control of the body changes, that is referred to as 'switching'. If the two personalities involved in the change are not co-conscious, switching can be very abrupt. If the two personalities involved are co-conscious, the change may be smoother and is termed 'shifting'. If more than one co-conscious personality simultaneously shares executive control of the body, they are referred to as being 'co-present'. (*Shifting* and *co-present* are terms which seem have originated with psychiatrist Colin Ross).

What is DID?

People with DID have multiple alters, who have distinct characters which may be similar or different to the host personality. Alters can be adults or children. In a fragmented state, the alter in control of the person's consciousness – their perceptions, thoughts, feelings and actions – can switch unpredictably. Switching can be triggered by a range of factors, for example, stress, anxiety, a set of terms or raised voices. Also in a fragmented state, these alters do not share memories, so the person can find clothes in their wardrobe they don't remember buying or wake up with injuries they don't remember sustaining. The common origin of DID is severe, repeated abuse in childhood.

The experience of each person with DID is unique. Behaviours linked to DID typically manifested early in life, commonly in adolescence. Some people are diagnosed and accept their identity in adolescence. Others are not diagnosed until mid-life, and before that developed coping mechanisms to navigate life while hiding their identity. A parallel is the way in which adults who are illiterate have developed effective and subtle ways to conceal the fact. Unless they are in acute distress, many people with DID go about their lives without acquaintances, colleagues or even friends being any the wiser. There are people with DID in many walks of life.

The goal of treatment of DID is to reduce the extent of fragmentation of the psyche. The success of treatment varies depending on the individual and the severity of the childhood trauma. At its best, the fragmentation can be healed or greatly reduced.

What about being AB?

Like DID, the experience of every AB is unique. It covers a large range. Some identify as diaper lovers (DLs) who wear diapers/nappies, but do not acknowledge any other attraction to the trappings of infancy or early childhood. Adult babies are attracted to nappies, and to the trappings and fantasies of infancy – with a repertoire of baby clothes, stuffed toys, pacifiers, bottles etc, that varies with each individual. ABs often refer to their baby or child side as their 'Little' and to inhabiting their baby side as 'little space'. For either DLs or ABs, the attraction can be exclusively sexual, exclusively for emotional comfort without a sexual dimension, or a combination of both.

The attraction to nappies commonly first manifests at an early age, even before adolescence. There is a strong involuntary dimension to the attraction. It is a deep need. Attempts to suppress it for any period commonly result in the involuntary triggering of an urgent and compelling need to put on a nappy.   Attempts at suppression also create a 'binge and purge' cycle with sharp, tumultuous and involuntary shifts in mood and behaviour. Conflicted ABs are typically adept at disguising these attractions and behaviours, even from those closest to them. The behaviours and fantasies are commonly incomprehensibly at odds with the adolescent or adult personality of the AB, and a source of deep shame and confusion that seeps into many aspects of the AB's life.

Some DLs and ABs come to terms and accept this side of their personality in adolescence (particularly after the advent of the internet and social media age). Many, especially those who grew up in an earlier age, remain deeply conflicted well into mid-life. There is often a high level of denial amongst ABDLs – of the amount of space their 'Little' occupies in their psyche, its' origins and its' implications.

DID on the Dissociation Spectrum

DID is the most extreme form of dissociation.

Dr Steinberg indicates people with DID typically have all five components of dissociation, and to a high degree. Amnesia, not just for past trauma, but for the activities of different alters in the present, is a defining characteristic of DID.

The Adult Baby – An Identity on the Dissociation Spectrum

The DSM-5 is the current version of the Diagnostic and Statistical Manual of Mental Disorders - the standard diagnostic tool published by the American Psychiatric Association (APA). It states the following criteria must be met for an individual to be diagnosed with DID:

1. The individual experiences two or more distinct identities or personality states (each with its own enduring pattern of perceiving, relating to, and thinking about the environment and self). Some cultures describe this as an experience of possession.
2. The disruption in identity involves a change in sense of self, sense of agency, and changes in behaviour, consciousness, memory, perception, cognition, and motor function.
3. Frequent gaps are found in the individual's memories of personal history, including people, places, and events, for both the distant and recent past. These recurrent gaps are not consistent with ordinary forgetting.

The symptoms cause clinically significant distress or impairment in social, occupational, or other important areas of functioning.

The differential diagnosis for DID excludes symptoms directly caused by other medical conditions (ie. seizures) or substances (ie. a drug of abuse or medication).

Essentially, the DSM-5 definition says DID is a combination of identity alteration and amnesia. For the purposes of the DSM-5 definition, these two components also subsume the other three identified by Dr Steinberg (identity confusion, de-personalisation and de-realization).

Dr Smith makes clear the link between identity alteration and amnesia –

The Adult Baby – An Identity on the Dissociation Spectrum

"The term 'multiple personality' does refer to the most striking feature of the disorder, but it also misplaces the emphasis. The key to making sense of dissociative identity disorder is to look not at the personalities but at the memory barriers between them. We could describe a house in two ways, either as a collection of rooms or as a collection of walls. Both are true, but one cannot construct a house out of rooms. Only walls can be constructed, and rooms are the result. When we first confront multiple personality, we see dramatically different personalities before our eyes. We see rooms, and it is easy to forget that their existence is really a consequence of there being walls – that is, dissociative memory barriers resulting from trauma. As memory barriers become fixed and are maintained over time, the personalities on opposite sides develop separate histories, values, allegiances, possessions and relationships. ... A consequence of the development of memory barriers is the development of sharply different personalities that diversify even more over time and are capable of vying for control over the body they inhabit."

Even with DID, denial is common. The ISSTD's 2010 Guidelines states -

"Clinicians should bear in mind that some persons with DID do not realize (or do not acknowledge to themselves) that their internal experience is different from that of others. In keeping with the view that dissociation may serve as a defense against uncomfortable realities, the presence of alternate identities and other dissociative symptoms is commonly denied and disavowed by persons with DID. This kind of denial is consistent with the defensive function of disavowing both the trauma and its related emotions and the subsequent dissociated sense of self."

The Adult Baby – An Identity on the Dissociation Spectrum

Overlap Between DID and AB

The DSM-5 criteria let us see clearly the relationship between DID and being AB. There is a strong overlap. A conflicted AB matches three of the four DSM-5 criteria for DID.

ABs fit the first DSM-5 criterion for DID - *"two or more distinct identities or personality states (each with its own enduring pattern of perceiving, relating to, and thinking about the environment and self)"*.

ABs fit the second DSM-5 criterion, notably the change in behaviour – *"The disruption in identity involves a change in sense of self, sense of agency, and changes in behaviour, consciousness, memory, perception, cognition, and motor function."*

ABs do **not** fit the third DSM-5 criterion – *"Frequent gaps are found in the individual's memories of personal history, including people, places, and events, for both the distant and recent past."*

Conflicted ABs *can* fit the fourth DSM-5 criterion – *"The symptoms cause clinically significant distress or impairment in social, occupational, or other important areas of functioning."*

We need to look further at the four criteria.

Conflicted DLs and AB's may consider they don't have a distinct child alter – it's just a 'side' of their otherwise adult personality. That may be true. In an earlier quotation, Dr Steinberg refers to moderate levels of identity alteration involving 'personality fragments' rather than distinct personality states with persistent traits and behaviours.

Conversely, for many ABs, I suspect the non-acceptance of a child alter represents unconscious repression, conscious denial, or the early stage of coming to terms with their confronting identity. For people with DID or ABs, often the personality of alters doesn't emerge from the sub-conscious until after self-acceptance (refer to Chapters 8 and 10 on alters). Before that, the alters influence behaviour, but largely from the sub-conscious. There are parallels with other minority identities where people don't accept their non-conforming sense of self until mid-life. That can happen even where they have kept secret over a long time, behaviours and thoughts which pointed towards that non-conforming sense of self.

Behaviour may be a more objective indicator of whether an AB fits the first two DSM-5 criteria for DID (an alternate personality, manifested behaviourally). For ABs, the extent of persistent involuntary behaviour commonly includes –

- a frequent irresistible compulsion to wear nappies - often triggered involuntarily;
- a deep need for non-sexual emotional comfort from nappies, pacifiers, bottles or the like;
- strong behavioural and mood swings linked to the 'binge and purge' cycle;
- a rich fantasy life deriving emotional comfort from identifying as a helpless or dependent baby, and being babied by caregivers and substitute parents.

We need to focus further on the 'binge and purge' cycle because it is the clearest indication of identity alteration for ABs. The phrase comes from the disease bulimia where the sufferer gorges on food and then, in deep self-disgust and loathing, makes themselves sick until they purge their stomachs empty. For adult babies, it means something different. It means bingeing on a new or extra stock of nappies and often other baby clothes and paraphernalia. Sometimes the binge is downloading digital AB erotic fiction.

The binge prompts recurring bouts of increasingly compulsive masturbation, perhaps fueled by psychologically unhealthy, masochistic AB fantasies. Like the bulimic, the binge causes initial euphoria and then deep self-loathing, which in turn results in a compulsive purge. The AB disposes of their entire stock of nappies and other AB supplies and vows to give up being AB forever. They may delete the digital copies of AB erotic fiction. There is an initial euphoria at being 'cleansed' of something bad. But after an interval, the AB's unmet needs for the comfort of nappies and baby fantasies kicks off another binge and the cycle reboots. The cycle is emotionally wrenching and exhausting.

The Adult Baby – An Identity on the Dissociation Spectrum

Both the binge and purge are involuntary. Having been through the cycle before, the AB's adult self is fully aware, but their executive control of decision making and physical action is over-ridden. In the *binge*, the over-ride is by a part of the psyche that is desperate for the comfort of nappies. In the *purge*, the over-ride is by an opposing part of the psyche that is terrified and repelled by these infantile needs and behaviours.

The binge and purge cycle and other involuntary AB behaviours fit Dr Steinberg's definition of "severe identity alteration, ... [which] involves a person's shifting between distinct personality states that take control of his or her behaviour and thought." That suggests a distinct child alter, whether acknowledged or not. Such behaviours fit the first and the second DSM-5 criterion for DID.

In terms of the third criterion – amnesia – ABs do not lose memory in the present or the recent past. They only have amnesia in terms of the repression of old childhood trauma and the origin and existence of the alter(s) which split during the trauma. Any alters which do emerge are fully co-conscious. Thereafter, sharing memories, the alters and the birth personality influence each other's traits and behaviours.

In terms of the fourth criterion – distress or impairment – conflicted ABs are intermittently tormented by the involuntary behaviours described above. The see-saw conflict between their adult and child selves constitutes 'identity confusion', one of the five components of dissociation. At its worst, such as the height of the binge and purge cycle, it represents distress and impairment.

The affinity between DID and being AB is illustrated in Dr Steinberg's statement -

> *"In the most basic terms dissociative identity disorder, or DID, formerly called multiple personality disorder, is what happens when your 'inner child' or some other hidden part of yourself operates independently, seizes control, and makes you act inappropriately or impairs your ability to function."*

46

The Adult Baby – An Identity on the Dissociation Spectrum

As an AB I can certainly recognize a lot of myself in Dr Steinberg's description. I suspect many other ABs would also.

I believe being AB is similar to DID, but without the amnesia.

It is interesting that women are far more likely to be diagnosed with DID than men, while ABs are far more likely to be male than female. The DSM IV-TR, the penultimate version of the Diagnostic and Statistical Manual of Mental Disorders, indicates DID is diagnosed three to nine times more frequently in adult females than adult males. I suspect the prevalence of the genders in both identities is more evenly balanced, and gendered patterns of behaviour conceal this. Women are more likely than men to seek assistance from mental health professionals, and less likely to disclose in often fetish-orientated AB forums and groups.

Being AB on the Dissociation Spectrum

I believe being AB is next door to DID on the dissociation spectrum. Let me explain.

I completed the diagnostic questionnaires for each of the five components of dissociation in Dr Steinberg's book. It indicated, in my conflicted state as an AB, I had moderate levels of identity confusion and identity alteration. I also had moderate levels of depersonalization in the form of detachment from my emotions and my body, and a sense of being a witness as much as a participant in my own life. But these latter sensations are not uncommon for emotionally avoidant, inhibited males. I have no significant derealization (experiencing the environment or others as unreal). Importantly, I have no amnesia. All my alters are co-conscious, they share present memory. In the absence of amnesia being AB is a sub-DID part of the dissociation spectrum.

The fact that some of the intermittent turmoil related to my conflicted AB identity did not ever result in medical intervention and a clinical diagnosis is, to some extent, a fortunate accident. In less advantageous circumstances, it might have been different. If I

The Adult Baby – An Identity on the Dissociation Spectrum
had been accurately diagnosed with a dissociative condition using the current DSM-5, it would likely have been *Other Specified Dissociative Disorder* (OSDD). I would fit the traits described by Dr Ross –

> *"Many people with chronic, complex dissociative disorders do not have full DID. In DSM-IV they had DDNOS [Dissociative Disorder Not Otherwise Specified], while in DSM-5 they have OSDD (Other Specified Dissociative Disorder). These are partial forms of DID in which the parts are not so distinct and separate, there is no full amnesia, or there is more co-presence [shared sensation and control of the body] than full switching. Sometimes the person has full DID, but the whole picture hasn't emerged yet, in which case OSDD is used until the picture does become clear." [Treatment of Dissociative Identity Disorder: Techniques and Strategies for Stabilisation]*

> *"... a patient may have several distinct personality states, but not have dissociative amnesia." ['Be a Teammate with Yourself: Understanding Trauma and Dissociation.']*

The Wikipedia article *Dissociative Disorder Not Otherwise Specified* indicates "DDNOS is the most common dissociative disorder and is diagnosed in 40% of dissociative disorder cases."

The ISSTD's 2010 Guidelines state -

> *"A substantial proportion of the dissociative cases encountered in clinical settings receive a diagnosis of DDNOS. Many of these DDNOS cases are well described by the DSM–IV–TR Example 1 of DDNOS: "Clinical presentations similar to dissociative identity disorder that fail to meet the full criteria for this disorder" ... There appear to be two major groupings of such DDNOS-1 cases: (a) full-blown DID cases whose diagnosis has not yet been confirmed (via the unambiguous manifestation of alternate identities) and (b) complex dissociative cases with some internal fragmentation and/or infrequent incidents of amnesia ... Patients in this latter group of DDNOS-1 are "almost-DID." DDNOS-1 patients are typically subject to DID-*

48

like disruptions in their functioning caused by switches in self-states and intrusions of feelings and memories into consciousness. Because these latter phenomena are often more subtle than cases with florid DID, it may require more skill and expertise on the part of clinicians to discern their presence."

ABs fit in category (b). As we have seen above, ABs have distinct personality states that manifest intermittently in behaviours which persist over a long period and are consistent in their character. But ABs do not display amnesia, except for the repression of the original trauma.

Blogger Rob Spring on the website PODS (Positive Outcomes for Dissociative Survivors) suggests OSDD/DDNOS can be distinguished from DID by a lesser level of trauma and lesser number of alters -

"In terms of other differences, it seems that as a general rule the degree of the trauma or attachment difficulties leading to DDNOS will be less severe than people who are diagnosed with dissociative identity disorder ... People with DDNOS may, for example, have had some 'good enough' attachment experiences or other mitigating factors. ... "

According to Van der Hart et al's structural model of dissociation (The Haunted Self, 2006), dissociative identity disorder is a case of tertiary dissociation with multiple ANPs [Apparently Normal Personalities] and multiple EPS [Emotional Personalities], whereas DDNOS is a case of secondary dissociation with a single ANP and multiple EPs. ['DID or DDNOS: does it matter?' cited in the references]

The last paragraph is saying something important, but the wording is a bit obscure. It is saying DID is the third, highest level of dissociation with multiple adult/functional personalities and multiple child/dysfunctional personalities. OSDD/DDNOS is the second, next level of dissociation with one adult/functional personality and multiple child/dysfunctional personalities. The latter characterization fits ABs.

The Adult Baby – An Identity on the Dissociation Spectrum

To consider ABs' place on the dissociation spectrum, we can look at the size of three populations.

1. The first is people with substantial dissociative symptoms – they are estimated to represent 10% of the total population.
2. The second is people with DID – they are estimated to represent 1% of the total population (a subset of the first group).
3. The third group is ABs – they are estimated to be one-in-a-thousand or 0.1% of the total population.

The estimated size of these populations does not prove but is consistent with, ABs being a subset on the sub-DID part of the dissociation spectrum. (If these orders of magnitude were reversed it would prove being AB could not be on the dissociation spectrum).

The Psyche is Wired Differently

I said in the introduction ABs that realize at some point their psyche is hard wired differently from everyone else they know. When I started this book, I thought of that in terms of the psychology of ABs. But I found several expert medical references which open the possibility it may be literally true, in terms of key structures in the brain. The two articles are from 2006 and 2008, the former from the American Journal of Psychiatry. They are cited in the references and discussed in greater detail in appendix 1.

The articles indicate when the brains of people with DID were imaged with magnetic resonance imaging (MRI), they show discernible differences from 'healthy' people. The 2008 article found people with DDNOS, those next door to DID on the dissociation spectrum, also had discernible differences when their brains were imaged. As discussed above, I believe ABs fall into the DDNOS/OSDD category. On this basis, it may be literally true the brains of ABs are hard-wired differently from singletons.

The articles are concerned with several key structures in the limbic (emotional) system in the brain – the hippocampus and the amygdala. The hippocampus has important roles in relation to memory - spatial memory that enables navigation, and decision making in uncertain circumstances (according to the Wikipedia article of the same name). It seems the size of the hippocampus can be affected through life by factors such as trauma and stress, medication and perhaps long term psychotherapy. The amygdala has a primary role in memory, decision-making and emotional responses (including fear, anxiety, and aggression) (again, according to the Wikipedia article of the same name). There are two of each structure, one on each side of the brain.

Smaller hippocampal volume has been reported in several stress-related psychiatric disorders, including post-traumatic stress disorder (PTSD), borderline personality disorder with early abuse, and depression with early abuse. The causal relationship between trauma and the size of the hippocampus is unclear. Is the smaller volume caused by trauma, or are people born with a smaller volume more vulnerable to trauma? The relationship between early stress and accompanying psychiatric disorders to amygdalar volume is even less clear.

The two articles suggest the people with DID had 19-25% smaller volumes in the hippocampus. This compares to a study of Vietnam War combat veterans with PTSD which showed a 20% reduction in volume compared with veterans having suffered no such symptoms (cited in Wikipedia). Other studies have suggested people with Borderline Personality Disorder have a 13-21% smaller volume for the Hippocampus than healthy people.

The 2008 article indicated people with DDNOS had 14% less hippocampal volume than healthy people. This would put them about midway between the people with DID, and 'healthy' people. It indicated otherwise the DID and DDNOS groups were similar, with both having 10-12% less volume in the amygdala, and 19-20% less volume in another key structure, the parahippocampal gyrus (which serves as an interface between structures in the limbic brain), than the healthy control group.

We need to be cautious about what we infer from the above. Both articles indicated when they were written in 2006-8, they were amongst the first research into the neurobiology of DID. They are based on small study populations. We don't know if the symptoms of the DDNOS study group resembled those of ABs (identity alternation rather than amnesia). I have no knowledge of neuroscience. I don't know how significant the differences in brain structure between the three populations are in terms of influencing cognition and behaviour. For ABs, I am not inferring any kind of behavioural determinism from those differences, or any diminution of personal responsibility. We need to acknowledge ABs share the vast majority of their psychology with everyone else. What I do take from the articles is a tentative basis for the idea the different wiring in AB's psyches may be neurological rather than just a matter of psychology.

It is important but confronting to realize that people with DID have never had a 'normal' unitary psyche as adolescents and adults. The childhood trauma which gave rise to their DID generally occurred at a young age, before the teenage years. From that point on their psyche has taken a divergent track. The ISSTD's 2010 Guidelines for Treating Dissociative Identity Disorder in Adults states -

> *"In short, these developmental models posit that DID does not arise from a previously mature, unified mind or "core personality" that becomes shattered or fractured. Rather, DID results from a failure of normal developmental integration caused by overwhelming experiences and disturbed caregiver-child interactions (including neglect and the failure to respond) during critical early developmental periods. This, in turn, leads some traumatized children to develop relatively discrete, personified behavioural states that ultimately evolve into the DID alternate identities."*

The 2006 article cited above states –

> *"Accordingly, the disorder [DID] has been conceptualized as a childhood-onset posttraumatic developmental disorder."*

I suspect this description is also largely true for ABs.

Childhood Trauma

So, if being AB is a form of identity alteration, there must have been childhood trauma where an alter split within the psyche. My book '*The Adult Baby Identity – A Self Help Guide*' describes the likely scenario for such trauma -

> "*Based on my experience I believe that there was a time, or times, in your childhood when you felt very frightened and desperately alone. You were a very young, vulnerable child. You felt overwhelmed. That was when the child persona emerged in your psyche. It was the best thing your psyche could do to protect you from despair.*
>
> *It does not have to mean that you had bad parents. Even with the best will in the world parents can't always protect their children from the 'ordinary catastrophes' of childhood. Those catastrophes include a young child being very frightened at a temporary separation from their mother or primary caregiver. But whatever it was, at the time you did not understand what was happening. You felt alone and unloved. And like all children who feel unloved, you felt it was your fault. You felt unlovable. Your Inner Child was wounded. And such childhood wounds stay with us. For some ABs, these wounds may not come from the ordinary catastrophes of childhood, but from abuse or neglect.*"

Rosalie Bent refers to the prospect of ABs recalling repressed trauma–

> "*Have you ever forgotten an important or traumatic incident that happened a long time ago and then suddenly, something triggered the memory and it came flooding back and was almost news to you? It happens to a lot of us at times and it happens to a Little One even more. The reason for this could be because Littles were often formed in their very young years and memories of that time seem to get filed in a dusty corner of the brain and forgotten as a matter of course.*

The Adult Baby – An Identity on the Dissociation Spectrum

Your Little One has as much access to all the adult's memories as the adult himself, right? Well, maybe not – it might be more. I don't want this to sound too overwhelming, but it is sometimes true that your regressed Little One might be better able to tell you about things in the past that were traumatic, than the adult. This might not always be a good thing, as some traumas are better left hidden, unless you are ready and able to deal with it. I bring this up though, because it may happen that your Little One dredges up an old memory from his distant past and it may or may not be related to how the regression began, or some other aspect to it." ['There's Still A Baby In My Bed: Learning To Live Happily With the Adult Baby in Your Relationship]

Validation

For ABs, the parallels with DID offer an important validation of their sense of self.

ABs are commonly mystified and confounded at the source and power of their compulsive demand for nappies. That is explained when we understand the power of alters within the psyches of people with DID. To describe alters as subjectively real doesn't adequately convey their power to affect a person's behaviour and bodily sensations. I have read references by mental health professionals to switches between DID alters where a person can go from displaying an allergy to having no allergic reaction; where medications will show greater or lesser or no effects; to presenting with convincing symptoms of physical maladies and then these quickly disappearing; or to experiencing pain or not from obvious physical wounds. These shifts are associated with switches between alters which do not share memories or even a knowledge of the other's existence. This does not apply to ABs, but it does indicate the power of the subjective experience of an alter to shape sensation and behaviour. If you doubt the power of subjectively real alters, read any autobiography of someone with DID (see Chapter 7).

The Adult Baby – An Identity on the Dissociation Spectrum

As we have seen, subjectively real alternate identities are accepted as a valid phenomenon by authoritative diagnostic texts like the DSM. They are acknowledged as having real and significant effects on a person's sense of self.

Admittedly, the validation in the DSM is 'backhanded'. It's in the context of a catalogue of mental disorders. But it's a start. And it's based on work like that of Dr Marlene Steinberg which indicates identity alteration is only one of five components of dissociation. Identity alteration by itself is not debilitating (as we shall see in Chapter 11). As the DSM indicates, identity alteration alone, in the absence of distress or impairment, is not a mental disorder. In this sense, I think of AB's as the lucky kids on the dissociation 'block'.

ABs can also take validation from two other key perspectives from mental health professionals working in the field of dissociation. Firstly, alternate identities have their origin in childhood dissociation. That validates the obvious point that the AB's obsession with nappies and the other trappings of infancy points to origins in issues and unmet needs in childhood. Secondly, enlightened mental health professionals accept psychological health lies in accepting these alters and having a cooperative relationship with them – not denying them (for example Dr Yeung's approach to DID – see his books cited in the references).

A Note on the Book 'There's Still A Baby in My Bed'

Rosalie and Michael Bent's book *'There's Still A Baby in My Bed: Learning to Live Happily with the Adult Baby in Your Relationship'* was the first published work to consider being AB as a personal identity, not a sexual fetish. It is an evergreen book of groundbreaking courage. It helped me enormously in coming to terms with being AB.

The book describes a comprehensive list of AB traits and symptoms which are indicative of, or consistent with, ABs being an identity on dissociation spectrum. I refer to many of these citations in this book. Rosalie and Michael use the terms regression or regress where I use the term dissociation or dissociate. But I believe we are describing the same phenomena. The book has a firm grasp on the nature of co-conscious alters. It represents a remarkable feat of insight – to deduce a dissociative identity from observation and first principles.

Rosalie and Michael's book states being AB is not Multiple Personality Disorder (or DID as MPD was renamed). This is absolutely true. However, it also says being AB is *not* dissociative. I interpret this to mean being AB does not involve dissociative *amnesia*. This book affirms that view.

I believe the position in *'There's Still a Baby in My Bed'* can be readily understood. It was the first book to take issue with the offensive, harmful and empirically inaccurate categorization of being AB as a paraphilia (a sexual fetish) in the DSM. That categorization groups being AB with flashers, gropers, peeping toms and paedophiles. In seeking to rescue AB's from the harm of this error it would have been a doubtful gain to give the impression being AB was the same as MPD/DID.

Now, with the benefit of the cumulative understanding initiated by Rosalie and Michael, we can understand the breadth of the dissociation spectrum. And being AB and DID can be on that spectrum, and share much in common (alters), while also being very different (ie. ABs don't have amnesia or a fragmented psyche).

Summary

There is an important overlap between DID and being AB. DID is a combination of identity alteration and amnesia. Being AB is similar to DID, in that it is identity alteration without the amnesia. The identity alteration is common to both. Being AB fits the category of Other Specified Dissociative Disorder (OSDD). That puts it next door to DID on the dissociation spectrum.

5. Regression

If being AB is a small subset of the much larger population with substantial dissociation symptoms, why does that manifest as a need, obsession and fetish for nappies? That isn't true for all the other people in the broader dissociative population.

I believe that's where regression comes in.

In regression, a person reverts to behaviours and a psychological state from their biological childhood. Those behaviours and states are not random. They represent points where the person's childhood development got stuck for a time, experienced difficulty or missed a step. This is referred to as a *fixation*. Most people have witnessed or read of situations where a young child, faced with an overwhelming crisis such as being hospitalized, separated from a parent, or the like, reverts to behaviours they had previously grown out of – bedwetting, thumb sucking, etc.

I suspect that ABs had issues, delays or setbacks in their continence and toilet training in childhood. I did. I posit the AB's regression to that point of fixation becomes the means by which a dissociated child alter breaks through from the unconscious and influences behaviour. The child alter is trying to signal both its existence and needs to our adult selves from behind high walls of repression, and later denial. The fixation with toilet training or bedwetting is the first hole in the wall.

There is no way of proving this hypothesis, but it fits with what we know about ABs. We know that the initial fetish for nappies typically blossoms eventually into a much larger repertoire of AB expressions and needs. That is consistent with the dissociated child alter eventually breaking through the hole in the wall of repression. Given the comparative rarity of ABs, it also makes sense there should be overlapping causal factors.

Okay, but why do we need to explain being AB in terms of dissociation at all? Why can't it be explained purely in terms of regression?

The Adult Baby – An Identity on the Dissociation Spectrum

There are four key facets of being AB which regression alone cannot adequately explain (and dissociation does). These are –

1. Key traits and preferences of the AB's 'Little' or child alter were often not part of the AB's biological childhood.
2. An AB's Little typically manifests over time as a multi-layered persona consistent with 'identity alteration', one of the five elements of dissociation, rather than a set of disparate regressive behaviours.
3. Conflicted ABs commonly experience 'identity confusion', one of the five elements of dissociation, typically a conscious duality and conflict between an adult and child self.
4. For ABs who have accepted their identity, the positive experience of self-nurturing their Little is not adequately represented by the concept of regression.

Each of these aspects is discussed below.

Not Reversion to Biological Childhood

An AB's 'Little' commonly has important traits or preferences which were not part of their biological childhood. These are better explained as belonging to a dissociated alter which is a sub-conscious, and later conscious, construct of the AB's psyche.

A good example is that many ABs identify with having a Little with a different gender from their biological childhood. Rosalie Bent indicates -

> '... around half of physically male Adult Babies and Little Ones identity as female infant/toddler, indeterminate or sissy. ... 'Sissy' and 'girl' are quite similar and when determining your Little One's gender, keep in mind the sissy option. It is a subset of the female gender, but for simplicity, I have used it as a separate one.'

Some of these ABs did identify as female at an early age and hence regression might encompass baby girl clothing and behaviours. I suspect most did not identify as female at an early enough age for those characteristics to be caused by regression to their biological infant or toddler state. In my case I have a baby girl alter but my biological childhood was exclusively male, and in a family with an absolute demarcation between gender identities. For me, a female child self could not be the result of regression to any part of my biological childhood.

It is likely many of the traits and preferences of AB's child selves do not faithfully replicate those of the AB's biological childhood. This does not deny that some of the constructs of the baby/child self are influenced by the AB's biological childhood. But this influence is mixed with others, at least as strong, which come from elsewhere in the psyche. That is more consistent with a dissociated alter, rather than regression.

Identity Alteration

An AB's Little typically manifests over time as a multi-layered persona. It's not just wearing nappies. It's also a wardrobe of baby clothes, pacifiers, stuffed toys, perhaps bottles, and activities such as watching children's TV, colouring books or playing with dolls. And the physical manifestation of the Little is only the tip of the iceberg, on top of a large repertoire of fantasy involving an imagined life as a baby. This goes well beyond a limited number of disparate childish behaviours such as might be linked to regression.

The manifestation of such a multi-layered persona is more consistent with a dissociated alter. That represents 'identity alteration', one of the five components of dissociation. The AB's Little is sufficiently elaborated as an alternative personality they are often named by the AB. Again, that is consistent with a state experienced by the AB, not as a set of disparate behaviours but as an alternative personality.

The Adult Baby – An Identity on the Dissociation Spectrum

Identity Confusion

Before AB's accept themselves, they typically experience an intermittent sense of turmoil and doubt about their identity. That experience is commonly one of living with dual and conflicting selves – the adult and the child. Even when the Little is denied by the AB, it is still experienced as a disruptive force which could unexpectedly manifest in the 'binge' part of the 'binge and purge' cycle, or in involuntary triggering of the need to put on a nappy. This is consistent with 'identity confusion', one of the five components of dissociation. This pervasive experience of uncertainty about identity is consistent with dissociation, rather than regression.

Self-Nurturing

When an AB accepts their identity, their episodes of 'baby time' (wearing a nappy, dressing in baby clothes, and the rest) represent self-nurturing of the AB's Little by the AB's adult self. That nurturing heals the AB's childhood wounds and supports a stable and healthy identity. The positive character of the AB's ongoing self-nurturing is more consistent with shared consciousness between an adult self, and a baby/child alter. It is less consistent with regressing alone to a past wounded biological childhood. Regression can be understood as a temporary psychological refuge when normal coping mechanisms have failed. The adult state is supplanted by a child state, and the former is not 'present' to comfort and protect the latter. Given the extent of Little related behaviours and traits in the lives and characters of ABs, that would suggest that ABs were neurotic failed adults. This is not consistent with the fact ABs are both sane, functional adults *and* experience themselves as subjectively real children.

On the basis of the above, I believe regression alone is insufficient to explain being AB. The conjunction of dissociation and regression is a good fit with what we know about ABs, and the breadth of AB traits and behaviours.

6. Dax and Dylan

It is time to introduce Dax and myself.

Dax has DID and I am an AB. Dax is my wife's nephew by marriage, from a previous marriage. Our chance acquaintance offered the opportunity to compare our experience of ourselves with a depth and honesty that would otherwise not be possible.

Dax

Dax is one-of-a-kind, a larger-than-life personality. This is reflected in both his character and sometimes tumultuous life course. He is a gifted teacher. He has taught children with learning difficulties with an empathy derived from the challenges he faced through his life. He has held senior positions in schools around the world and has a successful online consultancy business.

Dax describes himself as 'a fully functioning cognitive adult who embraced his DID. He chose a profession and way of life that allowed for periods of hospitalization, therapy and isolation without it impacting his attempts to lead a normal life.'

Into his forties, he was a devotee of extreme sports and visiting remote exotic places. He has climbed mountains in most continents, and run marathons in the arctic and on the Great Wall of China. Dax has 'a thing' for islands. It led him to spend three weeks alone on a remote uninhabited island off the south coast of Australia and to make his current home on a beautiful small island in the Caribbean.

He grew up in the United Kingdom, where, as a child, he was subject to severe and repeated physical, sexual and psychological abuse. He found love and understanding with an adoptive family and was diagnosed with DID at age 16. In therapy, he began the process of getting to know his alters. Tragically, his beloved first wife died in a car accident and his adoptive parents died shortly afterwards. His birth personality contracted another marriage

The Adult Baby – An Identity on the Dissociation Spectrum

without the knowledge and agreement of other alters. The marriage was unhappy and ended in separation. It produced two daughters whom Dax has supported financially into independent adulthood.

In the latter half of his life, Dax moved jobs and locations around the world every couple of years as his DID fractured relationships. Now aged in his early fifties, he has married his partner and has a baby. He believes he will settle on his beloved island home.

Dax has nine alters. There are others but these are shadowy non-verbal 'presences', felt, rather than known. The nine are represented in a distinctive tattoo on the back of his hand – a spiral in circles and dots. It is a touchstone to remind all his alters, in the midst of amnesia, of his identity. Though Dax had an early diagnosis and therapy, the deep childhood trauma means debilitating amnesia is always present in his life.

All Dax's alters are male. He has one child alter, little Dan, aged 7. The others are adults or teenagers. Dax is the host, but not the birth personality (more on that topic in Chapter 11). The capabilities Dax needs to successfully navigate the external adult world are spread between several key alters – Dax, Jonah, Jinx and Ollie. Dax is the facilitator and lead; Jinx handles money and logistics; Jonah handles strategy and planning, and Ollie is the athlete and enabler.

Dax's life is the story of a unique journey and of unique courage. We are now working on his autobiography.

Dax on DID

The most compelling perspective on DID comes from Dax's verbatim descriptions. Dax speaks in the plural, speaking for his 'system' of multiple alters.

> *"DID for us is not having more than one personality, it is one personality that is divided into parts. It is inaccurate to conceptualise us as having 'multiple personalities'. A more helpful conceptualisation is that we have access to less than*

one personality (at any one time). Living with DID means our parts are separated from each other by dissociative barriers. As a result, we have developed separately and have very different skills, opinions, memories, friends, history, preferences from each other. For example, we have different ages, sexual preferences, skills, interests and beliefs.

I will always remember having this explained to me like a delicate vase being dropped onto the floor. It can be repaired, but the pieces never fit properly back together.

Living with DID is both a pleasure and a curse. We celebrate our individuality but the cost lies in our relationships with others being fragmented.

Diagnosis was a relief, but definitely not a badge to wear with honour. It has hindered our life at every stage and should never be used as an excuse. It is what it is, DID is a condition that provides a unique perspective on life but at the same time one that limits achievements. We had to accept the conflict that DID brought into our life, failure to do so would have resulted in suicide or institutionalization.

However, as DID took a greater hold on our life, the degree of self-doubt diminished as we learnt to become self-reliant as the roles of the alters evolved. Through embracing DID and not letting it rule our life, we became more self-sufficient.

Many years ago we got described as high functioning and able to hide in plain sight. So now we are invisible, alive but suffering in silence, in full view but alone."

I suspect many ABs will relate to Dax's observation about hiding in plain sight.

Dylan

By contrast, except for being AB, I (Dylan) am boringly conventional. I am in my late fifties and happily retired from a senior position in government service. I have been married for over thirty years to my wife, the love of my life. Through marriage, I have grandchildren and great-grandchildren. I was born, bred and have lived my whole life in a State capital in Australia. I had an insecure attachment with my parents as a child but this was not the result of abuse or neglect.

I first experienced behaviours linked to being AB - a compelling need to wear nappies and fantasise about being babied - around age ten. Being AB caused intermittent turmoil in my life but never became a clinical issue. For the greater part of my life, I experienced being AB as a sexual fetish with compulsive behaviours that tyrannized my life. It was completely and inexplicably at odds with my inhibited, responsible adult self. Early on I thought marriage would 'cure' me. Later, I tried many times to give it up, with willpower and therapy. It always came back, ultimately stronger than before. I was in my forties before I reluctantly accepted it would never go away. I was in my fifties before I accepted being AB was a personal identity with a subjectively real child alter originating in childhood trauma.

My principal alter is a baby girl, Chrissie. She originated from a traumatic temporary separation from my mother when I was aged three or four. This is described in my book *"Living With Chrissie: My Life as an Adult Baby"* -

My mother went to a sporting club, presumably for some much-needed respite from caring alone for two small children. While she was playing I was left with my sister in the care of other adults. My sister became inconsolably distressed at the separation. I felt responsible, either for caring for her or at least for showing a good example. But in the face of her distress, I couldn't contain my own and ended up bursting into tears and wetting my pants. I couldn't see my mother and she seemed to have gone beyond hope of return. I felt terrified, overwhelmed and abandoned. I had failed to be the 'big boy' I was expected to be. My sister was picked up and comforted by the other adults but I don't remember being so comforted.

The Adult Baby – An Identity on the Dissociation Spectrum

I have two other child alters, boys, shy Joey and tough Robbie. Both are aged about nine or ten, my age when they split from my psyche. Joey originated from a traumatic fear of drowning, as described in my book -

> My parents placed great importance on me learning to swim ... I had a fear of water, especially of putting my head under the surface. I had not been successful at government-run holiday swimming lessons that were a rite of passage for kids of my generation. My parents enrolled me for private lessons with a brusque, intimidating male instructor [I was physically afraid of men] ... It was the middle of winter. We were forced to jump into the deep end of a cold unheated pool. I desperately wanted to be brave but I was terrified. I thought I was going to die. My parents persisted. I would wait with mounting terror for the time for the next lesson to roll by. I remember being driven crying and distressed to early morning swimming lessons in the winter rain. Eventually, they relented and I was sent to a psychologist. Evidently, on his advice, I was allowed to give up swimming lessons until I was ready for them several years later.

Robbie is the clearest example of a 'split' in my psyche. He originated from a traumatic bullying incident at primary school. It occurred on an oval out of sight of the main school complex. At breaks, it was only frequented by the older boys, unsupervised by teachers. It was 'Lord of the Flies' territory and you never 'dobbed'. I recall being alone and being circled by a large group of my taunting classmates. I blanked out, completely. When I recovered my senses I was sitting on top of a smaller classmate on the ground with my hands around his neck. My recollection is if I hadn't been pulled off by some older boys I would have strangled him. I was deeply shocked at my loss of control and what I was capable of. In the next several years I refused to fight again, even when I was hit by boys who were smaller than I was.

I have described these incidents to illustrate the 'ordinary catastrophes' of childhood can be sufficiently traumatic to lead to 'splitting'. In each incident, there were circumstances in my life at the time which may have increased my psychological vulnerability to trauma. Notwithstanding these childhood incidents, I grew up to become a strong-minded adult, capable of showing both physical and moral courage and leading others. I cite that to show I was not traumatized as a child because of an intrinsic weakness in my character. Trauma can briefly overwhelm a younger child's capacity to cope, no matter what that child's character.

Why didn't I understand as an adult, the impact of these traumatic incidents? In the case of the first incident, when I was aged three or four, it was part of family history and I had a visual recollection of the event. I always recalled the other incidents but buried the feelings associated with them. It was only after I talked to a skilled therapist in later life I recalled my emotional memory and joined it with the visual memory. Only then did I understand how traumatized I had been in each case. Therapy started the process of healing the trauma carried by my alters. Self-acceptance and the acceptance of my wife carried that healing through.

Accepting Chrissie as a real, fundamental and healthy part of my psyche has transformed my life. I feel whole, contented and safe in a way I never did before. That extends beyond my AB side to my life in general. Chrissie is a delight to me.

> *"Sure she can be a real 'little miss', at her worst a selfish brat. But she's also a shy, easily scared, innocent, loving, affectionate, warm-hearted, fun-loving little girl who melts my heart. My adult-self feels very good about comforting and protecting her."*

I now embrace being AB as a liberating and redeeming personal identity. My wife does not act as Chrissie's mother or caregiver, but she accepts Chrissie as subjectively real and can laugh with and about Chrissie, in ways that are deeply affirming and healing to me. Now, in retirement, there is a kind of 50:50 balance between my adult self and Chrissie. I sleep each night and spend each morning dressed as Chrissie in a nappy and baby clothes.

Stage of Life When We Accepted Our Identities

Dax and I consciously accepted our identities at different stages in our lives. For Dax, that was in young adulthood, and for me, it was in late adulthood. In this, neither of us is necessarily representative of our identities.

Both people with DID and ABs can accept their identities either early or late in their lives. Dax is representative of people of either identity or any minority identity, who do so early in life. I am representative of people with any minority identity who reach acceptance only later in life.

For Dax, the extent and effects of childhood abuse resulted in medical intervention early in his life. He was clinically diagnosed with DID aged 16 by mental health professionals and experienced that diagnosis as a relief from uncertainty. Conversely, there are many people with DID who do not accept their identity until mid-life, and some who never accept themselves.

I did not accept being AB as a minority personality until I was aged in my mid-fifties. This is despite showing the first behaviours linked to my identity (craving nappies) as early as age 10 and seeing therapists in relation to these behaviours several times as an adult. Conversely, there are many ABs who accept their identity as adolescents or young adults. This pattern has become much more prevalent with the advent of the internet and social media age.

The balance of this book explores what it feels like to live with DID and being AB, based on the experiences of Dax and myself. It points to when it feels similar, and when it feels different.

7. DID Autobiographies

No individual is representative of an entire identity – whether DID or AB. I had an awareness of where my circumstances and traits fitted within the broader ABDL population. I didn't have the same awareness of where Dax fitted within the DID population. To seek that awareness, I read case histories and five autobiographies of people with DID that covered a breadth of different circumstances.

The five autobiographies are summarized below -

Robert Oxnam was a prominent US and international academic leader whose career in Asian studies brought him into contact with the US President and business leaders like Bill Gates and Warren Buffett. His DID emerged in mid-life as he recovered from alcoholism and bulimia. His DID was caused by childhood physical, psychological and sexual abuse by men and women within his extended family. His first marriage ended before or during the early stages of treatment of his DID. His second wife, another prominent academic, accepted his DID and lovingly embraced his alters. He was 'outed' with DID and seems to have had to start a new career as an artist.

Before and after accepting his DID, he seems to be a self-important, grandiose and self-absorbed personality. Robert describes a dramatically gothic, compelling interior landscape peopled by his alters. His psychiatrist promoted fusion of his alters. Robert's account focuses on his treatment journey which led to eleven original alters integrating into three. He describes how his host personality switched from an alter back to his birth personality. He embraced his alters. One of the remaining triumvirates of healed alters was a child, and another a woman. His autobiography is 'A Fractured Mind: My Life With Multiple Personality Disorder'.

Christine Pattillo is an everyday woman from the northwestern US who earned her livelihood in the retail and financial services sectors. Alone of the five autobiographies cited here, she was consciously a multiple from childhood. She was not diagnosed with DID until crises in mid-life caused her to seek treatment. Her DID originated with physical and psychological childhood abuse from her father and childhood sexual abuse from a person outside her family.

Before her DID, she seems to have been a warm but deeply conflicted personality, suffering from sometimes debilitating bouts of anxiety, self-harm and bulimia. After accepting her DID, she is a warm, vibrant, optimistic personality. Her loving husband was at her side throughout her therapy. Her altruistic therapist emphasized cooperation between alters rather than fusion. She warmly embraced her alters who include children and a male teenager. Her remarkable account has the voice of the host/birth personality, each alter, and the host's husband and mother. It vividly describes her alters' characters and their relationships with each other. She lives openly as a 'multiple' and her husband embraces her vibrant, healed alters as his family. Her autobiography is '*I Am We: Living With Multiple Personalities*'.

Olga Trujillo was a high powered lawyer in the US Justice Department and later became an influential advocate for survivors of child abuse. Her DID emerged in mid-life. Both it and the memories of childhood abuse came as a complete and shocking revelation. Her DID was caused by a childhood of depraved, sexual, physical and psychological abuse by all members of her family. Her psychiatrist seems to have pursued treatment which emphasized abreaction – re-experiencing the trauma. She was re-traumatised over an extended period and her marriage to her loving husband did not survive. She later married a gay partner who accepts her DID. Before and after accepting the DID, she seems to be a highly controlled person focused on her work. She seems to have a functional, impersonal relationship with her alters. Her final relationship with her alters is unclear. Her autobiography is '*The Sum of My Parts: A Survivor's Story of Dissociative Identity Disorder*'.

The Adult Baby – An Identity on the Dissociation Spectrum

Herschel Walker is the most highly visible person I know who has come out as having DID. He had a highly successful career as a running back in the US National Football League (NFL) and as an Olympic athlete. He was one of the highest-paid NFL players in the 1990s. His DID emerged in mid-life as he grappled with the end of his NFL playing career and difficulties in his marriage. He recounts his life from childhood, describing how his at-the-time unrecognized alters helped him overcome being an overweight, stuttering child to become a superstar athlete. After his career finished, without an outlet for his competitiveness and aggression, his alters became dysfunctional. He entered therapy, but his marriage ended in divorce.

Alone of the five autobiographies cited here, his DID was not caused by sexual abuse or abuse within the family. He attributes it to a temporary separation from his mother after birth, but mostly to prolonged bullying and ostracism in primary school (he also witnessed a terrifying assault by hooded KKK thugs as a six-year-old). Before and after accepting his DID, he was a highly controlled, emotionally-avoidant person. He seems to have a functional, impersonal relationship with his alters. He doesn't refer to any child alters or alters of a different gender. His psychiatrist seems to have aimed for fusion of his alters. His autobiography is 'Breaking Free: My Life with Dissociative Identity Disorder.'

Cameron West is an everyday person from the US who was a prosperous small businessman before his DID. It emerged in mid-life after a debilitating crisis with his physical health. His DID was caused by childhood sexual abuse by his mother and grandmother. His loving wife had a background in working with special needs children and supported him through his diagnosis and recovery. Alone of the five, he had a young child when he was diagnosed with DID. His account focuses on his therapeutic journey and shows his struggle with denial. His therapists did not purse the fusion of his alters. His alters were co-conscious from the outset but switched uncontrollably.

71

The Adult Baby – An Identity on the Dissociation Spectrum

Before and after accepting the DID, he seems to be a warm empathic person. Both he and his wife warmly embraced his alters, especially his child alters. His alters included an adolescent girl. He lives as a multiple with a remaining core group of healed, mainly child alters. After his DID was diagnosed he reinvented his working life. His autobiography is *'First Person Plural: My Life As a Multiple'*. It was publicized by Oprah Winfrey.

I hope these brief sketches show people with DID come in many guises and walks of life. Each of them showed inspirational courage in facing repressed memories of abuse, and coming to terms with a new and challenging identity that their hidden pasts had foisted on them. They represent people you might work with or meet every day. I refer to their experiences throughout the rest of the book.

There is an implicit bias in these five accounts. All the people survived torment, found therapists who understood dissociation, and in varying degrees, healed themselves, to be able to publish their stories. Psychiatrist David Yeung's 14 case histories provide a more representative range of outcomes for people with severe DID (see his book *'Engaging Multiple Personalities Volume 1: Contextual Case Histories'* cited in the references). For those with severe dissociation, it can be an unkind world, with unaccepting partners, relatives, and mental health professionals. Of those 14 who eventually found an empathic and skilled therapist in Dr Yeung, two committed suicide and three others remained at high risk with uncontrolled fragmentation. However, for the greater majority, an accurate diagnosis and effective therapy was a route to healing and psychological health.

8. Living With Alters

For Dax and I there is a compelling similarity in our sense of self. We both live with alters which are real to us, and which influence our perceptions, thoughts, feelings and actions on a daily basis.

The next three chapters discuss this common experience. The effects of amnesia shape living with alters in ways which are unique to DID. These differences will be discussed in Chapter 11.

The experience of living with alters which are common to both of us include-

1. how it feels to live with alters;
2. triggering;
3. alters' fundamental place in our psyche;
4. alters' effect on relationships with loved ones.

Each of these topics is discussed below.

How It Feels

Our alters feel completely real. They never go away, they are part of our psyche 24/7. People are familiar with this perspective on DID. It is also true for ABs. Rosalie Bent recognized these two fundamentals for ABs in her book *'There's Still A Baby in My Bed'*. Addressing the partners of ABs she says –

> *"The startling news for you is that the child is always there. ... In the case of your Little One, however, there is a very real Inner Child that is well-formed and accessible via deep regression."*

When an alter is 'out' – at the forefront of our consciousness – we experience the world in real-time through the lens of that alter's perceptions, feelings and thoughts.

When an alter is not 'out' they are always sitting in the background, each processing the same events and sense impressions according to their age and character (and in my case, gender). A sense-impression may have a different meaning for one alter than another. It is common for at least one alter to have the function of 'watcher'. Thus multiples always have more than one pair of eyes 'in the room' (or rather they process the same sensory stimuli from multiple viewpoints). This can be positive or negative. In the positive, it can mean multiples don't miss much when they focus. In an earlier quote, Dr Yeung referred to how teachers or therapists with DID can be exceptionally perceptive and sensitive to their students or clients. In the negative, when a situation triggers unconscious memories of past trauma, it can result in hypervigilance – being on high alert that can shade into high anxiety or a panic attack.

My principal alter, Chrissie, is deeply comforted by wearing nappies, and the familiarity of a wet nappy. Ditto for soft-to-the-touch, pastel pink, pyjama-style baby clothes. She loves an afternoon nap and calmly drifts into sleep on her back, comforted by her pacifier and with her beloved soft toys, Bunny and Dolly, cuddled on either side. Each night she sleeps soundly between child-patterned flannelette sheets and feels deeply protected by the presence of Bunny and Dolly. She has an instinctual comfort from the constant presence of an array of stuffed toys in her bedroom looking out at her when she wakes or goes to sleep. Her dolls set inspires a deep desire to play, cuddling and feeding her dolls. She has a spontaneous delight at seeing a pretty baby girl's dress or outfit, or an appealing soft toy.

This repertoire of feelings and reactions are completely at odds with my inhibited adult self. Yet I have slowly learned to trust their instinctual nature, consistency, and spontaneity as being real and honest. They are not an act or even my conscious imagination. They really do belong to a little girl in my psyche. My other alters, Joey and Robbie, are less prominent, but just as real.

It is the same for Dax. For him the experience of an alter who is 'out' is even more compelling because that alter is less aware all the others are also present in the background.

Whether an alter is 'out' depends on conscious choice, or whether the alter is 'triggered' by a sense impression (sight, sound, smell – a familiar or confronting situation). *Choice* is the optimal situation. For Dax, that means the adult alter with the capabilities most appropriate to a situation is 'out'. For Dax and myself, it means a child alter can come out to 'be' or play when it's safe and congenial. In this benign sense, it's not much different than a 'singleton' who shifts between different roles and contexts in their daily life.

A common experience is a person can have alters of a different gender from the host personality. This is prevalent in both identities. I earlier quoted Rosalie Bent saying about half of male ABs have a female/sissy Little. That's me. Colin Ross indicated in a sample of 236 people with DID, 62% had an alter of a different gender (cited in *'Dissociative Identity Disorder'* p151). In three of the five DID autobiographies, the author cited having an alter of a different gender. That can be true for hosts of any gender. Christine Pattillo gives a humorous account of being a middle-aged woman with an alter who is a hormone-driven male teenager. Some other people with DID, or ABs, only have alters with the same gender as their host personality. That is true of Dax.

Sensationalist accounts of DID often emphasize the high number of alters. ABs commonly identify as having one 'Little'. That can make it seem ABs must be completely different from people with DID. It is not so. If you have one alter besides your host personality you are a multiple. An experience of self, based on a subjectively real alternative personality, is still very different from an experience of self-based on a unitary psyche.

But sometimes ABs can also have multiple 'Littles' or alters. Rosalie Bent recognized this -

"Your Little One may be more than one! ... For example, a Little might have behaviours ranging from ages twelve months up to eight years old. In this case, they may separate into one, three, five and eight-year-old identities and have different names for each. They may have separate clothing preferences, toys and other objects. Their behaviours may range from a non-

*walking, baby-talking one year old, to an eight-year-old with
all the abilities and more of a typical child of that age."*

For people with DID, a large number of alters belongs to a highly fragmented state before healing. This can happen where a person is exposed to repeated trauma over an extended period. Dissociation and splitting become an established pattern to protect the psyche. The DSM IV-TR indicates males diagnosed with DID have an average of around eight alters, while females average fifteen or more. Some of the large number of alters may be what Dr Steinberg refers to as personality 'fragments' which are feeling states without a developed personality. Healing seems to result in some alters becoming inactive, fusing with others or disappearing. After the process of healing people with DID commonly seem to have a core group of alters numbered in the single figures – Robert Oxnam has 3, Christine Pattillo has 6, Cameron West has 9, and Dax has 6.

Triggering

Triggering is an involuntary process. People are used to talking about triggering for people with DID or Post Traumatic Stress Disorder (PTSD). It also applies to ABs. Rosalie Bent describes it as follows -

> *"A stressor or trigger occurs to begin the process. This may be an event, a sight, a memory or a sudden emotion. It can also be a smell or the presence of a specific object ..."*

> *"You need to become aware of triggers which can start a deep regression, rather than just a shallow one. Sometimes, there are triggers to avoid, such as baby shops, children's books or sights and smells that push regression into higher levels."*

Any alter can potentially be triggered any time, 24/7. It can be nice, such as when a child alter sees a friendly dog or an enticing toy, and spontaneously comes out to enjoy the experience. It can be confronting, such as when a situation prompts a feeling of threat, discomfort or distress, and suddenly you are experiencing your body and the world through a personality that may be agitated, angry or frightened. Other times it can be a strong feeling of unease and tension.

My triggering is now manageable. I accept the existence of my alters and understand their personalities and triggers. All are co-conscious, so while a single event and sense-impression can produce different reactions, all know what the others are experiencing. Mostly my host and alters are co-present, sharing the sensations and control of my body (more on this later). Outside of that, changes are more a case of 'shifting', a smoother and less abrupt experience than 'switching'.

It was far more confronting when I didn't accept and understand the nature of my identity. My alters held unrecognized and unhealed trauma from my childhood. At times that was like an emotional tinderbox waiting for a spark. Then the influences on my feelings, thoughts and actions, sometimes seemed capricious and unpredictable. I sometimes experienced abrupt switching. I can remember occasions in my adult life when I had to flee from social situations, desperately trying to disguise the incomprehensible panic of my unrecognized alters.

For Dax, the situation is far more difficult. His triggering is abrupt -

> *"When we switch it's fast, it's a blink, the click of the fingers and that's ...it my lights go out, although I have got to understand a lot more about the triggers that cause the switching..one second I'm conscious the next I'm unconscious. My next conscious thought maybe 4 hrs later or the next day or longer."*

Some of his alters are co-conscious with others, but others are not. Some of the alters live with childhood pain so deep it will never fully heal. As Dr Yeung indicates, they have PTSD. At its worst it's like 'flashbacks' for combat veterans – Dax's system can go from zero to full fight-or-flight mode in a heartbeat. He can be confronted by the reactions of others to words or actions by an alter that is no longer 'out', and have no recollection of their words and actions.

That is living with present-amnesia and makes triggering a sometimes-confronting experience.

Both of us can be plagued by symptoms another might take as chronic or acute anxiety. It might be construed as social anxiety, linked to apprehensions about interacting with others. But it's not anxiety in the way most would understand it. If you have alters who can be triggered involuntarily at any time, walking into a crowded bustling room of strangers can be the equivalent of trying to take a gaggle of skittish or boisterous dogs across a busy four-lane highway. That experience can be nerve-wracking. The 'anxiety' is a realistic apprehension of risk and potential difficulty.

Alters Are Fundamental

For Dax and myself, our alters hold indispensable pieces of our psyches. Dax uses an analogy of a broken vase to describe his psyche – each alter is a fragment of the whole. They have different, complementary roles. The alters also give Dax access to a different sexual orientation than his birth personality and represents that fulfilment of his psyche. For me, as an AB my child alters, kept the capacity for tenderness and innocent joy, alive within my psyche. It also allowed me to express an important female part of my psyche.

For Dax and myself, the character of our alters is not random. It follows an unconscious logic. For example, for both of us, the gender of key alter(s) is the one that is psychologically safest. All Dax's alters are male. Dax, the host, is gay. He experienced the most wounding psychological abuse in childhood from his biological mother, making males a safer gender. It is the reverse for me. There was no abuse or violence in my childhood but there were no safe, embracing male role models. As a child, I was emotionally estranged from my father and afraid of him.

Our alters are permanent. Some therapists believe the outcome of successful therapy is that alters are fused into the undifferentiated Self. Some people with DID follow that route. Conversely, many seem to retain their alters, but build cooperative relationships with them. That's the way it is for Dax and myself.

The Adult Baby – An Identity on the Dissociation Spectrum

What peace I have with myself is the product of a long process to accept my subjective reality. Each alter represents an indispensable part of me. Dax and I both experience a suggestion or expectation our alters will, or should, disappear, as negating our identity. (See the discussion on the different expert views of alters in Chapter 14).

Relationships With Loved Ones

Alters have a big impact on our relationships with those closest to us, and in turn, those relationships have a big impact on our alters. It's a two-way street.

For people with DID, and ABs, there are two important factors which are not present in most other peoples' relationship with their partners.

Firstly, alters are fundamental to how a person experiences themselves and life, and there is a vast difference between having to conceal that fact and being able to share it. A partner's acceptance of the subjective reality of alters is a big issue. The process of reaching that acceptance is just as confronting, complicated and lengthy as it is for the person with the identity.

Secondly, with the presence of alters, the partnership is not just a one to one relationship, it is one to two or more. The relationship dynamics can get complicated. This aspect is succinctly highlighted in the comment by Dr Yeung –

> *"For DID patients, marriage is very complicated. It is often the case that some alters are very fond of the spouse while others are not."*

There is an overlap between these two issues. For a partner who hasn't yet, or doesn't ever, accept alters are subjectively real, they are left with seeing their partner as 'bad' – moody, irritable, angry – or 'mad' – unstable, delusional etc. Even for an accepting partner, there can be a sense of loss for the person they thought they knew, bewilderment, and fear of where this is all leading.

The Adult Baby – An Identity on the Dissociation Spectrum

For some people, either with DID, or ABs, it doesn't work out well. In three of the five DID autobiographies, the author's marriage did not survive the diagnosis and early treatment of DID. Dax's partner loves and accepts Dax but prefers to think of Dax's identity as autism rather than DID. For Dax, that leaves a space and a yearning.

Dax's marriage to his beloved first wife is an example of where a loving partner accepts the subjective reality of alters. Of the five autobiographies of people with DID, two had loving partners who supported them through diagnosis and treatment, and two others had second partnerships with people who accepted their DID. Three of the autobiographies show the giant leap of empathy and imagination an accepting partner makes – they have a relationship, not only with their partner's host personality but also with each of their alters. My wife accepts and relates to each of my alters. For every accepting partner, this represents a gift of the deepest and most healing love.

The issues and relationships between a partner and child alters is a related - but distinct - issue. That is discussed in the next chapter.

Summary

Both people with DID, and ABs, are multiples. Our sense of self is intertwined with our compelling experience of our subjectively real alters. Those alters process our sensory impressions according to their own unique characters, traits and histories. Each of our alters influence, and are influenced by, our relationships with others, especially loved ones.

9. Child Alters – The Key Similarity

The most compelling similarities between people with DID, and ABs, can be seen in their child alters, and in the relationship between their child alters and their partners. These two aspects are discussed separately below.

DID Young Child Alters

<u>**Child**</u> **alters are the defining characteristic of ABs.**

But people with DID usually also have child alters. Dr Yeung says of the latter –

> *"Because the traumatic experiences occur primarily in childhood, child alters are almost always present. There are usually several of them. Each has his or her distinct characteristics and performs a specific function. ... Most child alters are locked in their ages and never grow up."*

The public view of DID commonly focuses on the number of alters, and does not grasp that child alters are often central to the psyche of functional people with DID. Their experience of their child alters echoes that of ABs.

Dax says of his child alter -

> *"Dan is a child, I think around around 7, he loves the color red and dinosaurs. He likes to paint and role play, has lots of different voices. I know he plays with Aaron [Dax's baby son with his partner] a lot."*

We have already met Christine Pattillio's six-year-old alter, Chrissy, in the second chapter. Christine also has a delightful two year alter, Cyndi. Her autobiography provides the following accounts of Cyndi by her mother, Christine herself, and another of Christine's alters-

> *[Christine's mother says of a two-year-old child alter] "Cyndi could not walk, barely spoke, and on occasions wet her pants –*

ie. Christine's pants. This was not good. My daughter is a grown woman who could at any provocation turn into an infant sucking her thumb. That was a hard adjustment, but the more time I spent with Cyndi, the more I was amazed at all her little nonsense songs, her funny little sounds, and how she breathes while sleeping, so clearly a young child. It's been extraordinary watching her."

[Christine says of Cyndi] "... Christopher, family and friends would try to let me know the minute I shifted back out after a visit from [by] Cyndi. Christopher would even videotape her and I would see myself singing and acting like a baby. I was mortified. I had visions of being out in public as this self-conscious, overweight, middle-aged woman sucking a thumb and peeing my pants. (Yes, Cyndi wasn't potty trained and we guess she was about two years old.)"

['Q' one of Christine's alters, a young woman with a speech impediment describes an incident with Cyndi] "One day I at a craft store getting supplies for my business. Cyndi need go poop. Cyndi hates going big potty and cries and cries. I walk us to the restroom and shift Cyndi out. While Cyndi crying, 'No Poo Poo Koo', someone else enters the bathroom. Nothing can do so just let Cyndi stay out and fuss. I can't potty for her. After a few minutes, I hear woman asking if Cyndi OK. Cyndi keep crying. Woman ask if Cyndi want her to go get her Mommy. I think fast and shift back out saying, 'No I right here. She just not like go poop.' The woman laugh and tell me her grandson same. Now Cyndi done, but sit and wait for woman to leave. Was not sure what she might think if only me walk out of stall and no physical child."

The child alters of people with DID are subjectively real young children with similar capacities for wonder and fun, and similar needs for love and protection, as young biological children. This is understood by empathic mental health professionals and in DID self-help books.

Dr Yeung says –

The Adult Baby – An Identity on the Dissociation Spectrum

"Child alters think, feel, speak, and sometimes write, as young children. This is how they see themselves, regardless of their chronological age. The therapist must refrain from judging or treating them as adults."

The DID self-help book 'Got Parts: An Insider's Guide to Managing Life Successfully With Dissociative Identity Disorder', says of child alters -

"Remember to love, to cherish, to value these young parts. … It can take great patience, finesse and wisdom to deal with wounded 'littles' … Yet, as they realise the 'bigs' in the System [psyche] will keep them safe, the rewards are well worth the investment of time and effort as they shed layers of fear and distrust and to learn to be open and loving and inquisitive and playful as they do their own healing work."

'Got Parts' goes on to discuss the need for an internal sanctuary within the mind, in terms which emphasize the needs of child alters –

"Within these guidelines, your 'dome' can contain within it anything that brings you all comfort, pleasure, peace and security. Do you want a reading area with a fireplace, an area to play or listen to music, a playground for the littles? Would you like to have a perpetual rainbow, or lots of soft, warm blankets and cuddly pillows, or a lake or pool to swim in? Would you like to have unicorns, hummingbirds, butterflies, or a gentle-to-the-System [psyche] but fiercely protective dinosaur? You may have it in your Dome."

There is a striking similarity in the character and needs of the child alters of people with DID, to the child alters of ABs is striking.

The autobiographies of Christine Pattillo and Cameron West are exceptional in the warmth and openness with which they embrace and describe young child alters – in Christine's case, a baby alter. I wonder if their experiences might be less exceptional amongst people with DID than they seem. To publish an autobiography about DID in the face of deep misunderstanding takes great courage. I wonder if others have self-censored accounts of the character and needs of their young child alters for fear of exacerbating the stigma and ridicule amongst the uninformed.

This supposition is supported by the following comment in a recent (2016) text for therapists on dissociation -

> *"It is not uncommon for patients to report they have infant dissociative parts. Often, very young behaviours are associated with the activity of these parts, such as thumb sucking, rocking and bedwetting." [Treating Trauma Related Dissociation: A Practical Integrative Approach]*

DID Child Alters and Partners

Subjectively real child alters are similar to biological children. Typically they seek love and acceptance from the host's partner. Dax's description of the relationship between his loving wife and his 7-year-old child alter affirms this -

> *"Amelia treated Dan like a loving protective big sister, with compassion and empathy. Dan's needs are simple, he needed to be shown kindness - being hugged, having a story read to him or just listening to music. Dan wanted someone to listen and help him understand why certain things happened."*

A partner's acceptance of the existence and needs of child alters was central to the happiness of three of the five authors of DID autobiographies.

For Cameron West, the turning point in his journey with DID was his wife Rikki's loving embrace of his child alters. She had understandably held them at a distance to protect the couple's nine-year-old son, Kyle. The breakthrough came in a conversation between Cameron, Rikki and Cameron's psychiatrist Steve, cited below -.

> *[Steve asked Rikki] "What if you agreed to spend time with Cam's alters, say in the evening after Kyle's gone to bed. Give them some time out in the house. Help them feel accepted ...*

not just by saying that they are, but by being with them. In exchange, we could ask them to wait until Kyle gets a little older before they meet him.

"What I'd like to do, Rikki," Steve continued, "is talk with Cam's alters, in particular with Clay [8 yo alter] and the other young ones, and see if they'd be willing to kind of watch out for Kyle and be his protectors, and know that you'll be their friend and protector after Kyle goes to bed and he's not around."

"Steve, that's an excellent idea," Rikki said excitedly. "I'd be happy to spend time with Cam's guys. I'd do it every night. ..."

[Cameron] Suddenly the world was in color again. Inside Clay was telling Per yes, he'd do that, he'd be Kyle's protector, and Switch [8 yo] was saying the same thing, and Wyatt [10 yo] too, they were puffing their chests out like they were the new sheriffs in town. And Dusty [12 yo girl alter] was even saying she'd like to be able to talk to Rikki. ...

She said, "I promise to talk to everyone at night after Kyle's gone to bed."
"Oh God, Rik", I [Cameron] said, tears forming in my eyes. "That'd be wonderful."

She said, "I want everyone inside to know that I'd appreciate it tremendously if they'll kind of watch out for Kyle and go in when he's around, at least until he's old enough to understand a little better. And I'll be their friend and talk to them when he's not around, even if it's during the day. Okay?"

Then Clay switched out and said in his little voice, "Okay. L-like a sheriff, right Rikki? To watch out for Kyle."

Rikki laughed. "Yup, Clay. Just like a sheriff." ['First Person Plural: My Life As a Multiple']

After being tormented by her DID Christine Pattillo arrived at a place of happiness and contentment based on the warm

85

acceptance of her alters, especially her child alters, by herself and her loving husband Christopher. This is described below -

> *[One of Christine's other alters, says] "Most nights, it's Cita [Christine Pattillo] who is physically shifted out and sleeping in bed next to her husband. The rest of us snuggle down in our own beds [in the sanctuary in Christine's mind]. It is common for the two youngest, Cyndi the [2 yo] baby and [6 yo] Chrissy, to shift out and say their goodnights to Christopher."*

> *"… it's as harmonious as it gets for us. That is, until Cyndi, the youngest alter, all of about two years old, wakes and shouts, "Pee Pee Poppi, Pee Pee!" ("Poppi" is Christopher.) Then of course, one of us is shifting out and taking us to the restroom before Cyndi takes a leak in Cita's pyjamas. Yes, that has happened a time or two. …"*

> *Christopher says of Chrissy – "If I gently touch her arm she'll continue to sleep, but then she quietly says, "That's My Christopher." If I tickle her, she busts a gut laughing. She won't wake up and I'm warmed by her own special giggle. I feel as close to her then as if I'm sitting right next to her in her internal bedroom. Chrissy has an extraordinary ability to touch my heartstrings, the high pitches and low tones that no one else can play.*

> *But he also had to work extremely hard on his patience:*

> *Christopher: I was now a first-time father and I had to learn to reach her on her own level. Chrissy's feelings were easily hurt and there were times when I would accidently squish them. I was learning how to be around a small child. I became aware of how frightened she became when I sounded too harsh or used profanity." ['I Am We: My Life With Multiple Personalities']*

Robert Oxnam, a more controlled and status focused person, also cites his second wife's loving embrace of his alters, especially his child alter, as a turning point in his life.

The Adult Baby – An Identity on the Dissociation Spectrum

AB Child Alters and Partners

We can compare the above accounts with several from the partners of regressive ABs.

The first is by 'Kayley' and refers to her AB husband's 'Little', a toddler named Jenny -

> "It took me a long time to connect with my husband's toddler inner child especially since she is a girl inside! At first it seemed like I would never find her and he would never find me, but eventually, we connected, and things just started to happen. ... Jenny bubbled out all this stuff about his own mother who was distant and uninvolved and how he felt cheated out of a mother. ... He cried for hours as he just dumped all this raw emotion onto me about never feeling properly loved. ... it was pretty clear that he wanted me to pretty much assume a genuine step-mother/adoptive mother with him. ... I decided to informally adopt Baby Jenny as my daughter and then set about working out how to do it. ... Since then the relationship has just blossomed. I think by adopting her I now feel free to be her mommy in every aspect when she is a Little. And when she is my husband again I still feel this special bond that extends beyond the norm. ... as far as we are concerned, Jenny is my REAL daughter and we wouldn't have it any other way. A new complication arrived a year later in the form of twins. But even though I have real children, I still have a child who is every bit as real to me, and while the twins will grow up and out, Jenny will not. My daughter is mine for good. ['There's Still A Baby in My Bed' – Case Studies]

The second is by the wife of an AB named 'Joe', and refers to her husband's Little, 'Joey' -

> "... He also very slowly and carefully let me know he has a thing for diapers. ... I did understand where it was coming from as I know the extremely long history of abuse that started when he was 2 years old. The other tell tale sign that this had a

87

much deeper cause was the frustration fits that were thrown. Joe would get so mad and worked up when he was stressed that he would basically throw a temper tantrum. If I managed to get to hold him he would calm down and snuggle into me. He would put his thumb in his mouth and curl up with me and stay that way for up to an hour sometimes. This was the start of me understanding his deep need to regress especially after a wet lap a few times.

Some people may not believe in regression, but Joe is two different personalities. It isn't as far as a multiple personality, but a toddler version of him. Knowing it has had more than its challenges, but also benefits to both of us. His two big conflicts where admitting he had a need to regress and dealing with how deep his need for diapers is. It became much more obvious to me how much happier and relaxed the adult Joe was when he had a diaper on. It made a huge difference in our relationship and his stress levels. The diapers seemed to tie both worlds together. Joe accepts that there is a little inside and Joey feels that he is accepted and has a place in our lives and a tie to the outside world." ['There's Still A Baby in My Bed' – Case Studies]

In the above account, Joe's wife rejects the idea his Little represents multiple personalities. I suspect this echoes the views of many other ABs and their partners. It reflects a misunderstanding that only people with DID / MPD have alters. As we have seen, this is not the case. It is notable the account includes key features of a dissociated identity – childhood abuse and trauma; and a personality distinct from Joe's adult self which manifests beyond conscious control, with its own infantile needs.

In her groundbreaking self-help book for the partners of ABs, Rosalie Bent says -

"There is a very special kind of relationship that can exist between a loving couple, where one of them is a regressive adult baby, or what I call a 'little one'. ... It is what I call the Parent/Child relationship and it is where you have a deep,

The Adult Baby – An Identity on the Dissociation Spectrum

meaningful and substantive relationship, not just with your adult partner, but also with their Inner Child (or Baby) as well. ... The Parent/Child relationship operates at two basic levels. In the primary level, you will relate to your partner as adult to adult, just as you do right now. The secondary level is where you relate to your Little One as a child or infant, with you as their parent.

If there is one aspect of the Parent/Child relationship that is truly unique, it is the depth of interaction that can eventuate from it. Within a functioning Parent/Child relationship, there can be a level of communication between two souls which can be truly unique and exquisite. ... Rather than treat regression as a curse, it should be treated as an opportunity to have a relationship that combines the very best of both worlds [ie adult to adult; adult to child] ... ['There's Still A Baby in My Bed']

My wife and I now accept my alters. She is not a mother or caregiver to my alters, but more like a kind and fun-loving aunt. I don't have to hide my alters and she is no longer afraid of my identity. That is wonderful - liberating, healing and life-changing. I have greater contentment and happiness than at any previous time in my life.

Similarities In Relations With Partners

There are compelling similarities between people with DID and ABs, in terms of relations between partners and child alters.

In the negative, child alters desperately want love and kindness, but can be vulnerable, fearful and skittish. They will commonly quickly withdraw in the face of any sign of rejection by partners. (In the early days, those signs are typically of the behaviours of the child alter, rather than of their explicit existence.) The hurt and anger that comes from such interactions can be disruptive to a relationship and typically misunderstood by a partner as immaturity, petulance or moodiness. It can be awful for all concerned.

In the positive, a partner's acceptance of a person's child alters is transformative. There is a striking similarity between the two identities in the descriptions of a partner's acceptance. All these partners discerned their loving acceptance of their spouse's subjective reality was make-or-break for both their spouse's psychological health, and their marriage/relationship. In each case, the partner's acceptance was an act of courage, empathy and love.

The renown psychotherapist Donald Winnicott lets us understand how a partner's acceptance works psychologically. It fits with Winnicott's widely accepted concept of transitional phenomena. Things as diverse as a baby's security blanket, child's play, and all culture such as sports, politics and religion, belong to the category of transitional phenomena. Such phenomena are neither wholly subjective (solely inside the mind) nor wholly objective (physically tangible) – but somewhere in between. We can tacitly agree with others to invest shared activities with common meanings which are not inherent in objective forms. Winnicott says of transitional phenomena (here called 'intermediate' phenomena) -

> *"Should an adult make claims on us for our acceptance of the objectivity of his subjective phenomena we discern or diagnose madness. If, however, the adult can manage to enjoy the personal intermediate area without making claims, then we can acknowledge our own corresponding intermediate areas, and are pleased to find a degree of overlapping, that is to say common experience between members of a group in art or religion or philosophy." [Playing and Reality]*

For people with DID, or ABs, alters are subjectively real – to them. But if they insist that anyone else take that alter as objective reality ie. the same as a biological child or person, then people will perceive them as mentally ill (this is discussed in Chapter 15). However, a person with DID, or an AB, who is happier, more vital, because they have accepted their own subjective reality, invites a partner to share an intermediate or transitional space – where the person and their partner accept the alters are subjectively real to the former. That can be a healthy, happy space as per the above.

A Difference

There are many similarities between people with DID, and ABs, in terms of the relationship between their partners and their child alters. One difference is I did not come across any reference to power exchange in the relations between people with DID and their partners. Power exchange refers to dominance/submission practices where one adult sometimes exercises authority over a consenting partner in a manner outside normal, equal relations between adult peers eg. one person taking the parent role and treating the other like a child. Dominant Daddy/Little Girl (DDLG) is an example of a power exchange relationship. On-line many ABs seem to have or seek DDLG relationships – or the gender converse, variously identified as Dominant Mummy or Caregiver / Little Boy, or similar. These relationship patterns are found within and beyond the ABDL community.

I suspect the presence or absence of doubt is responsible for this difference between the two populations. People with DID have less cause to doubt the subjective reality of being a multiple with child alters. They will often have a diagnosis by a mental health professional. Prior to diagnosis and treatment, they and their partners will often have lived through the trauma of amnesiac alters with uncontrolled triggering and switching. After that DID is all too real. They have tangible indications they are dealing with a subjectively real child.

By comparison, being AB is regarded as a fetish or a kink. Those are labels which explain nothing. Both are pretty flimsy hooks on which to hang the challenging subjective reality of child alters who need regular nurturing for the AB to avoid becoming neurotic. So for both the AB and their partner, there is doubt about what being AB *really* is, and no model for the place of child alters in a partnership. I suspect some people fill in the gap with power exchange relationship models. Those are borrowed from sexual fetishism and bondage and discipline (B&D). Power exchange relationships become a vehicle for the acceptance and nurturing of dissociated child alters within a partnership.

The downside of power exchange relationship models is they further fetishize being AB through dominance and submission practices borrowed from B&D. Secondly, it can foster the perspective the AB's partner is the primary source of nurturing and parenting for the AB's child alter. In a psychologically healthy multiple that role belongs to the multiple's adult host (see the discussion in Chapter 15.) This is why it is important to understand being AB is an identity on the dissociation spectrum. It gives ABs and their partners greater capacity to choose relationship models which do not borrow inappropriately from fetishism.

Summary

The overlap between people with DID and ABs is strikingly clear in their experience of child alters. Some of the accounts of child alters I have read could be transposed from people with DID to ABs, or vice versa, and people of the other identity would not readily pick the difference. For both identities, a loving partner's acceptance of child alters is affirming and healing. It is often a turning point in people's lives.

10. Alters Don't Stand Still

Alters are subjectively real.

They are not metaphorical in the same way as the 'inner child' of a singleton. They have their own personality, their own perspective on life, their own needs, their own virtues and vices. Alters are an 'engine room' of the psyche of multiples. They drive change in our sense of self, and in what we want and get from life.

It starts with our alters breaking through the repression that kept them hidden in our sub-conscious. That forces us to come to terms with their existence and their needs. The dynamism continues after we have accepted ourselves as multiples. These processes of change are discussed below.

Coming to Terms with Alters

Coming to terms with our alters was a long and complex process for Dax and myself.

I believe people with DID, and ABs, go through the same stages of accepting their identity as other people with a minority identity. That process moves through stages of initial discovery and confusion, denial, ambivalence, reluctant acceptance, to full acceptance and pride, and hopefully, finally to a transcendent view which sees the commonalities across different identities. These follow the six stages of identity formation described by Dr Viv Cass in her widely accepted *'Theory of Lesbian and Gay Identity Formation'*. (See my book *'The Adult Baby Identity – Coming Out As An AB'* for a discussion of Dr Cass' theory and its application to ABs.)

For people with DID, and ABs, the different stages of identity formation can best be seen in their acceptance of their alters. Some, like Christine Patillo and Cameron West, end up warmly accepting their alters. They explore and celebrate their individual character, give them personal names, schedule 'out' time to enjoy activities, and share them with partners and close family. In short, they proudly celebrate their alters.

Others like Herschel Walker and Olga Trujillo seem more ambivalent. They appear to hold their alters at a distance. The alters' character remains an outline, defined only by their behaviours, or function or dysfunction in the psyche. The alters are given only functional labels like 'the consoler,' rather than personal names, or they are identified only by their age. This seems to apply even for child alters.

The difference between tolerating and warmly embracing alters seems to be reflected in the person's experience of life. Christine Pattillo and Cameron West's books show personal destinations lit by warmth, optimism and openness. This is despite overcoming earlier torment with their identities and childhood trauma. There is a kind of equality between their adult host personality and their alters.

The other autobiographies of people with DID are different. Their personal destinations don't seem as warm and buoyant. They seem to place greater emphasis on the outward control and success of the adult host personality, and hold the child alters at arm's length. Dr Ross refers to this phenomena as 'host resistance', and describes it as follows -

> *"The problem of host resistance is a frequent theme in the treatment of DID. ... the host personality often believes that she is 'the person' and the alters are second class citizens with no rights. This is a form of resistance. All the parts are parts of the whole – the host is just the part who has the job of being the host. There is only one person, but she is fragmented into parts who think they are separate from each other. ...*
>
> *The host commonly thinks that the alters are the problem, when actually they are holding intolerable feelings, conflict and memories so the host can function in the outside world. Also, often, they are reacting to rejection and devaluation by the host.*
>
> *"It is important to remind yourself that DID work is the same as work with a non-DID person, just broken into parts.*

The Adult Baby – An Identity on the Dissociation Spectrum

Developing empathy for the self, treating the self more kindly, accepting rather than avoiding difficult feelings, taking responsibility for one's actions, learning self-soothing, and so on, are basic recovery tasks for anyone. The same is true for people with DID."

ABs seem to span a similar spectrum in terms of their relationship with their child alters. That ranges from embracing to just tolerance.

Some alters can have dysfunctional behaviours. This is particularly so before self-acceptance and healing. There can be a fierce conflict between alters and some can be abusive and damaging to others. Christine Pattillo and Robert Oxnam describe how some of their alters would terrorise others. The abusive alters represented the internalized negative feelings from abuse or trauma. Often the child alters are on the wrong end of those conflicts. All of that is tormenting for the whole psyche. In my case there was a horrible three-cornered conflict between a punitive parent alter, my child alters and my adult host personality. (This is described in my book *'The Adult Baby Identity – A Self Help Guide'*.) Dax had similar experiences with his alters.

For Dax and myself, our alters held the trauma from the original events which led to their splitting from our psyches. For Dax, those are deep wounds from childhood abuse. Those wounds never fully heal. Dax has learned to live with them. Likely that is why amnesia continues to have such a large part in his psyche. Dax does not dwell on these matters, I believe because he does not wish to be defined by them. Instead, he focuses on living with his DID the best way he can.

For Dax and myself, psychological health came from accepting our alters as real, and building a cooperative relationship with them. Our alters influence our feelings, thoughts, actions, our sense of self, and our experience of the world on an hourly and daily basis. Not accepting something that powerful and pervasive within our own psyche would cause us psychological harm.

For Dax, with DID, that acceptance is literally a matter of life and death. He explains -

> *"Most, if not all, of the other DID sufferers we encountered over 30 years ago have died, some through old age, most through suicide. Many people fail to understand and integrate their alters. Most develop a psychosis that drives them mad. So their DID in a collective sense, consumed them."*

For both of us, getting to know our alters was a lengthy process. Alters don't jump out and announce themselves like the genie-in-a-bottle in Aladdin. Alters are a product of our sub-conscious. Before we accepted our identities, we experienced our alters only as disruptive, incomprehensible behaviours, at odds with our adolescent or adult personality. We didn't connect those behaviours with our alters. It was only after we accepted our alters as real that we could really start to get to know them. Each is as unique as our host personality. They are multi-dimensional with their own likes, dislikes, fears, 'hot buttons', virtues and vices.

Starting when Dax was diagnosed with DID as a teenager, with therapy and the support of his adoptive parents, he developed a cooperative relationship between his alters. He explains -

> *"There are 9 alters. Through a lot of therapy, support and hard work their roles have become very clear over the past 30 years. Each has a particular skill, trait or characteristic and is signified by the tattoo on my hand. The tattoo is a reminder that we are more than one..we are the sum of each of us. When the "Power of Nine" was built over many years, we were each asked to describe who we felt we were, each of us had therapy time explaining how important our roles where. I feel that it gave us a sense of responsibility that we respected because we were recognized. It took a huge amount of time and money to map through...lots of dead ends, negativity from the alters and silence.*

Enlightened medical professionals who accept the subjective reality of alters, recommend people with DID seek this kind of cooperative relationship with their alters. (For example, see psychiatrist David Yeung's books cited in the reading list.) Rosalie Bent urges the same approach for ABs, to accept and come to terms with their child personas.

For me, as an AB, accepting my alters wasn't a matter of death, but it was a matter of life - the difference between a happy fulfilled life, and neurosis. In the latter, doubt, self-loathing and anger intermittently but persistently tormented my mind, spirit, and marriage. Accepting my baby alter, Chrissie, as real, lead to positive and powerful cognitive and behavioural changes. I would never have anticipated the strength of those changes and the power of self-acceptance. The compulsive behaviours that formerly tyrannized my life disappeared. That includes compulsive masturbation, involuntary 'triggering', the 'binge and purge' cycle, a shopping addiction (for baby clothes), and psychologically unsafe fantasies. All gone! Try changing that with just will power (not happening)! In its place there is a comfort and safety with myself, that has extended to my marriage.

Having accepted my alters, I have looked back over my life with different eyes. I am beginning to see how, even when they were unrecognized, they played a big part in my experience of self and life. It's a bit like the way a person who discovers in mid-life they were adopted, looks back and re-interprets their life. Herschel Walker's autobiography is a good example of the retrospective application of this new perspective.

Alters Are Dynamic

For Dax and I, the presence of alters within our psyches changes and grows stronger through life. My reading suggests that is often true of people with DID, and ABs.

These changes are driven by three things –

1. the erosion of the repression that concealed the full presence and character of our alters;

2. changes in external circumstances, especially less necessity for concealment; and

3. self-acceptance.

Each of these is discussed below.

The presence and character of our alters are progressively revealed by the erosion of repression within our psyches. Childhood dissociation has a deep and pervasive effect on the psyche. The repression of dissociation in the unconscious breaks down very slowly, often over many years and decades, well into later life. The erosion of the repression does not proceed at a uniform pace. Crises in life, especially in mid-life, can suddenly release chunks of repressed memory and the expression of alters. But in my experience, rarely all of it at once. The rest, especially the full character of alters, continues to slowly come to the surface in an intermittent series of quietly surprising insights and subtle changes. Four years after the therapy where I first fully accepted my alters, this is still happening for me. Herschel Walker indicated it was still happening for him ten years after his DID was diagnosed. It was similar in Christine Pattillo's account.

Rosalie Bent, addressing the partners of ABs, discusses this dynamic in a manner I find consistent with the progressive emergence of a repressed alter -

> *"The truth of the matter is that the extent of the regression for a Little One does progress over time. ... The real question however is: does it expand regardless of what you do? And the answer is a qualified yes. The needs and behaviours of the Little are constantly evolving, even if sometimes quite slowly. Different circumstances develop different needs and wants. New experiences alter their feelings and perceptions. In short, like any biological child, your partner is changing. The difference is, that while a biological child matures, the Little One generally remains the same basic age. What does change, however, is the expression of that age. He will add new behaviours, modify others, and remove some altogether."*

The Adult Baby – An Identity on the Dissociation Spectrum

Change is also driven by our external circumstances. Our alters have been held back by fear and necessity. When those inhibiting factors abate, the presence of our alters grows stronger. Rosalie Bent recognized the extent and character of an AB's child self grows and develops over time, and it is often held back by circumstance rather than choice.

Felix Conrad in his book *'How to Jedi Mind Trick Your Gender Dsyphoria'* describes a parallel in the way external circumstances influence the expression of transgender people. He says the conformity involved in full-time, out-of-home work, conflicts with the expression of self for transgender people. That was also true of me as an AB. It is not just the constraint to present as 'normal' while at work. Mostly it was how that lifestyle suppressed, 24/7, the space in my psyche I could afford to give my alters. It was only after I retired from my job a few years ago that changed. My principal child alter, Chrissie, now takes a large space in my daily life in a way that would have been impossible before I retired. Only arriving at that point has created a feeling of a stable, safe and cooperative co-existence. Dax is currently on the cusp of shifting to working from home. The prospect of greater freedom for those of his alters that have had to stay more in the background, is both welcome and a source of concern.

The authors of four of the five DID autobiographies describe making changes to their careers after the diagnosis and acceptance of themselves as multiples. In part or whole that was to allow greater space and freedom for their alters.

Self-acceptance also drives change. In my case, I got tired of being hostage to fear about others finding out about my identity. I set much of that fear aside. I don't mean to court harm by 'outing' my identity in an unsafe way. But in the safety of my private life, I find happiness and contentment in giving space for my alters to be themselves – for me to be me. I am well into the second half of my life. I have a sense of *'if not now, when?'* I suspect that is true for many people with any form of non-conforming sense of self.

Living in an accepting household lets alters feel safe and express their personalities more. This is not just a conscious process. I can provide an example. When I was writing this book my wife spontaneously pointed out one of my latest mannerisms. Sometimes when I am standing, I find myself absentmindedly taking the sides of the hem of my T-shirt in each hand. With kind laughter my wife observed it was the sort of thing a little girl would do with her dress. It was initially completely unconscious on my part. Now I am aware, it feels very Chrissie (my baby girl alter).

Nature of Changes

The shifts described above, are in turn, reflected in changes within, and between alters. The changes can include -

1. some alters heal and transform positively;
2. some alters can disappear or fuse with another;
3. at the most extreme, the function of host personality can shift from the birth personality to an alter, or from one alter to another;
4. alters, singly and as a community, can 'relapse' to previous dysfunctional behaviours in the face of neglect, or denial by ourselves; and
5. alters can get out of balance, just like any biological personality.

Each of these is discussed below.

The most positive change is the way alters can heal with self-acceptance, the acceptance of partners or therapy. This leads to a transformation of alters from angry or frightened with dysfunctional behaviours, to being happy and settled. Christine Pattillo, Cameron West and Robert Oxnam describe such transformations and how that powerfully changed their lives for the better. Some had formerly harsh or angry adolescent or adult alters who transformed into protectors and nurturers of their child alters. They each had child alters who became sources of innocent joy. Christine Pattillo provides a vivid account of how those transformations were experienced by the alters themselves. I believe this trajectory can be seen for each AB who's life has been transformed by self-acceptance. When I didn't recognize or accept her, my baby girl alter, Chrissie, was alternately frightened and needy, or a tantrum-throwing brat. Now she is happy and content, secure in the knowledge she is loved and protected by myself and my wife. The change in Chrissie has transformed my life.

In the process of change, some alters can disappear or fuse with another. This is linked to the process of healing. How it plays out seems to be different for each person. Robert Oxnam describes how most of his original alters fused with the one's that remained, the positive capabilities of the former now accessed by the latter. Christine Pattillo describes how a beloved female alter passed away when her protecting and nurturing role was taken over by Christine as she grew stronger. Cameron West indicates now he has healed, some of his most wounded alters are rarely seen anymore. I suspect that after I accepted myself as a multiple and retired, an unnamed punitive alter that was focused on duty in my vocation has integrated or fused with my birth-host personality.

The extreme form of change is when the host personality changes. It can move to or from the birth personality to an alter, or from one alter to another. This is the case with Dax. It is not applicable to the vast majority of ABs. Yet it may be relevant in some rare examples. This issue is discussed in Chapter 11.

When there is a life crisis or a reversal of progress in self-acceptance alters can revert to former dysfunctional feeling states, behaviours and conflicts with each other. Alters are subjectively real. When they are neglected and disregarded they react badly. Robert Oxnam gives an example of how such a relapse undid much of the healing he had accomplished and threatened his marriage and his life.

Alters are also like any other biological personalilty, they go through ups and down, times when they are happy and content and times where they are selfish and 'off beam'. Remember our alters are present 24/7 processing the same sensory impressions and life experiences as our adult host. Life is a moving picture and our alters move with it.

For ABs, this dynamic is even more true of our child alters. Their senses, experiences and reactions can be more vivid than those of adult personalities. Self-accepting ABs love their Littles as the apple-of-their-eye. In the positive, they bring the joy and contentment of well-loved children. But sometimes, an AB's adult host can be overindulgent and over permissive, spoiling our child alters. And like biological children that can sometimes make them spoilt brats - greedy, selfish and demanding.

Summary

Alters are dynamic – they drive change in the psyches of multiples. That is clear in the process of coming to terms with being a multiple. But it continues after self-acceptance. As a multiple, we experience life through the kaleidoscope view of each of our alters. And each can bring change to our life as a multiple.

11. DID and Being AB Are <u>Not</u> The Same

We have seen powerful similarities between the two identities, but DID and being AB are NOT the same.

This chapter focuses on the key differences between the two identities. For Dax and myself, these include -

1. the origins of our identities;
2. the nature of the division in our psyches;
3. the complexity of relationships within our psyches; and
4. the psychological function served by our identities.

Let's look at each of these in turn.

Origins

There is a difference in the origin of Dax's DID and my identity as an AB. For Dax, DID had its source in severe and repeated physical, sexual and psychological abuse in childhood. Dax's experience is representative. The ISSTD's 2010 Guidelines states -

> *"DID develops during the course of childhood, and clinicians have rarely encountered cases of DID that derive from adult-onset trauma (unless it is superimposed on preexisting childhood trauma and preexisting latent or dormant fragmentation)."*

The DSM-5 indicates childhood abuse is present in 90% of people with DID (cited in the Wikipedia article on DID). Dax has learned to live with those wounds, but they may be too deep to fully heal. They leave a legacy that forever contests with hope and joy. The idea of suicide never completely goes away (for one or more of his alters).

The Adult Baby – An Identity on the Dissociation Spectrum

DID can have other childhood origins. For example, Herschel Walker cites a temporary separation from his mother after birth, and severe and prolonged bullying and ostracism in primary school, as the origin of his DID. (He also witnessed a terrifying assault by hooded Klu Klux Klan thugs as a six-year-old which may have contributed). Dr Yeung states –

> *"Deprivation of emotional support in a child's early years can constitute a passive type of severe abuse powerful enough to result in pathological dissociation."*

For me, the child alters that are my AB identity, came from being traumatized by the 'ordinary catastrophes' of childhood (as detailed in chapter 6). There was no abuse or neglect. Based on posts in on-line ABDL forums, I believe these ordinary catastrophes of childhood are a more typical origin for ABs than child abuse.

The Nature of Division Within the Psyche

Dax experiences DID as a pervasive fragmentation of his psyche. By contrast, before self-acceptance, I experienced being an AB as a conflicted Jekyll-and-Hyde duality. Fragmentation is a lot more damaging and difficult to heal than duality.

When I was conflicted, I experienced being AB as a competing dual nature – adult versus child. Was I an adult or a child? How could I be both? Did the baby side of me mean I was a failed adult? (For a full discussion of the symptoms of this conflict see my book *'The Adult Baby Identity – A Self Help Guide'.*) Although the duality could be tormenting at times, it was not fragmentation. The bugbear for me was identity confusion, not amnesia.

My only amnesia was the repression of the original childhood trauma and the existence of my alters. In the present, my alters are all co-conscious. I suspect it is the same for most ABs. Even when I was conflicted, I had the benefit of a consoling faith and a distinct sense of a higher self. I had only moderate levels of depersonalization and no significant derealization (experiencing the environment or others as unreal).

The Adult Baby – An Identity on the Dissociation Spectrum

My alters have distinct personalities. But there is some permeability between their character and my host personality. That's because memory is shared and the original trauma is largely healed. That permeability is shown in several ways.

Firstly, communication within my psyche is non-verbal - 'sensed' rather than heard. My alters are not so distinct from my host personality that I hear a concrete dialogue with them.

Secondly, my child alters influence traits in my adult host (and presumably vice versa). For example, my principal child alter is a baby girl, and my adult host now identifies much more with the perspective of women in politics. I have also come to prefer girls as the leading protagonists in the young adult fiction I like to read, and to write.

Thirdly, my adult host personality is *co-present* with my alters. That is a term used by psychiatrist Colin Ross to indicate both sharing the sensations and control of the body. For example, now I am retired I don't always shave every day. My adult male host self is untroubled by short bristly stubble but my baby girl alter doesn't like the feel or appearance of it.

This permeability is characteristic of sub-DID dissociation – OSDD (Other Specified Dissociative Disorder). Rosalie Bent identified this permeability (described as behavioural leakage or crossover) as a characteristic of ABs. For me, this permeability means the experience of living with alters doesn't feel fragmented. After accepting my identity, I experience being AB and a multiple as a loving internal family lead by my adult host.

Co-presence produces a different experience of alters in ABs than for many people with DID. Let me explain. In both identities, alters are present 24/7 and potentially can trigger and come 'out' at any time. For people with DID with amnesia, if an alter is 'out' it controls the thoughts, feelings, perceptions and actions of the person to the exclusion of the other personalities.

It's different for self-accepting ABs. Amnesia is not an issue. So once an AB accepts their 'Little', that alter is commonly co-present with the host. Co-presence also happens for people with

DID who heal their trauma. But the special character of ABs is their child alters are commonly very young – infants or toddlers. So the unique character of a self-accepting AB is co-habiting your body with an incontinent small child almost 24/7. The longer an AB has accepted their Little the stronger than sense of co-habitation grows.

I believe that explains why self-accepting ABs progress to wearing nappies for longer periods each day. Some ABs need to wear nappies 24/7. The co-presence of an incontinent toddler may have an adverse effect on continence (as with Christine Pattillo and her alter Cyndi) – although for many ABs the co-present adult self maintains continence. But whether continent or incontinent, wearing nappies for an extended period meets an emotional need. It is the need of the co-present child alter for a physical sensation which is familiar and comforting. This is true for me. I sleep every night and spend most mornings in a nappy. The co-presence of my baby alter also explains why the constant presence of a comforting array of stuffed toys in my bedroom, and the nappy bucket in the laundry, have such a soothing effect.

Because their psyches aren't fragmented, ABs are also less likely to experience an alter unilaterally taking executive control of their body from their host. That is generally uncommon for ABs, but it does happen. It happens in periods of high stress or triggering, probably related to the original trauma. The example of Joanne, the baby girl alter traumatized by a nighttime storm cited in Chapter 2 fits the latter circumstance. Before I understood and accepted myself as a multiple, I experienced these changes in executive control in the 'binge and purge' cycle or in confronting social situations (as discussed in Chapter 4). Curiously, I believe that the circumstance where ABs generally experience changes in executive control is sex (as discussed in Chapter 16).

Dax on Living With Fragmentation

In contrast, for Dax, every day is a struggle to pull the pieces of his fragmented psyche together. That fragmentation is driven by–

- amnesia which divides the real-time memories of some of the alters, and limits the cooperation between them; and
- derealisation and depersonalization, the sense the world and the self, respectively, are not real, caused by the amnesia.

This fragmentation is driven by the extent of his childhood trauma. Dax says of his amnesia-

"compartmentalised memory was our bodies response to memories that couldn't be processed. they are not forgotten, not resolved and will be forever with us. they hang over us like a hangman's noose!"

For Dax, that trauma is an insurmountable obstacle to faith in a divinity. He has a diffuse sense of his higher self. There is limited co-consciousness and no co-presence between alters. Dax experiences his alters as highly distinct from the host, and 'hears' concrete dialogues between alters. He says -

"... there is often noise, voices in my head. I tended to regard these as the alters talking but it could be my conscious, subconscious and co-conscious thoughts are fighting to be heard. Filtering them out is not easy and when it gets too invasive we tend to switch."

Dax's verbatim descriptions provide a compelling understanding of what it is like to live with a fragmented psyche.

"We switch about 4/5 times a day. This occurs when a situation becomes unbearable for the conscious alter, or there is a trigger that causes the switching or a change of environment, or the one most common to us on a daily basis, is the changing of roles due to the time of day. We have no idea, who will be conscious when. The concept of time means nothing. I refer to time as being 'present' and 'lost' time. I guess I'm [Dax] present maybe a few hours a day or not at all, depends on triggers.

The Adult Baby – An Identity on the Dissociation Spectrum

I have a fractured perspective of any given day, week, month; memories are broken, incomplete or not there at all (amnesia). As many of us are conscious over any given period of time, no one has the complete picture, emotional reactions are often missing or inappropriate decisions are made when only some of the facts are known to the conscious alter.

How do you stand in front of someone and tell them you have no idea what they are talking about yet they are adamant you had a conversation not 3 hours ago... trying to explain that it was with another alter, seems farcical, comedy to the extreme !!

So we are spectators in our own lives. Because nothing is real, we try to fill in the gaps by reading body language, guessing some responses or just passing over certain things or people as irrelevant.

Daily life is chaotic, disjointed and often it's hard to decide what was thought, what was a recalled memory and what is an action. So when I stress and worry, I was always taught to rehearse what you want to say but after lots of repetition and if the stress remains or the day ends for me, I never know whether that thought became an action and then a memory. Hence, this fugue state of existence means that most things seem unreal because you're never 100% sure that the action happened.

We are constantly detached from environments we should know and the people we interact with. Think of this as Groundhog Day occurring over several days/weeks. We don't relive the same day over and over but we do continue to make the same mistakes because we are disconnected, no one and nothing is familiar. It causes us to become distressed and in its severest form causes trauma.

Dissociation unplugs us from our own senses, dulling or even removing altogether our sight (I am often blind, unable to read or focus). De-realisation occurs often, where we feel totally disconnected from the world around us, it feels like being in a dream. Nothing feels 'real'. This may not sound so bad but it is very distressing.

Throw 500 jigsaw pieces in the air many times, each time they land you are left with a completely different pattern. That's what fragmentation is like for us. I'm trying to make sense of everything ..with a constantly changing set of data.

We are probably awake on average 16-18+ hours a day, consume massive amounts of information, are constantly trying to find ways to be safe."

Dax uses 'Post-It' notes to communicate between alters that are barely co-conscious. One alter will write a 'stickie' to another. Dax explains –

"these are simple messages, a few words, a song title, a keyword, a number, a cash figure....but rarely a sentence. Unfortunately, too often we ignore a message meant for us, so during the time of high volume interactions and at certain times of the year..it can fail as we simply forget.

We do not have any link or awareness of the actions of each other. These events are compartmentalized within each of us. If we have been respectful and followed protocol then someone will leave a " stickie" to prompt/ remind one of us to follow up on something. Let me explain – I [Dax] can make a conscious decision to drive to the shops, but I will not make the decision to go to the ATM and withdraw cash. Jinx is responsible and retains knowledge of codes, pins, passwords, internet access addresses..etc although I'm aware of the banking Apps on our iPad.

The experience of time loss due to amnesia and switching is characteristic of DID. Dr Yeung says -

"Most of us have experienced situations in which time seems to disappear, such as when we are driving long distances or deeply absorbed in something we enjoy. ... Qualities of time-loss characteristic of DID are different, and returning to the

ordinary experience of time is a terrifying jolt. After conventional experiences of time loss, we do not find ourselves with cigarettes in our pocket when we are confirmed non-smokers, nor are we greeted by people we do not know who obviously know us by a different name."

Dax's perspective lets us see how disorientating and painful this experience can be –

"We have no idea, who will be conscious when. The concept of time means nothing. I refer to time as being " Present" and " Lost" time. I guess I'm present maybe a few hours a day or not at all, depends on triggers. We never wear a watch or have any clocks visible on the walls. Clocks represent pain, isolation and loneliness."

Dax's experience shows it is the traumatizing effect of living with amnesia on a daily basis which drives de-personalisation and de-realisation. It is unhealed childhood trauma and the amnesia it produces, which is the debilitating component of DID, rather than identity alteration or alters, per se.

The Complexity of Relationships Within the Psyche

The relationships between alters within Dax's psyche are more complex than they are for me. In this, we are representative of our respective identities.

The relationships within my psyche are straight forward. I have three alters. They all 'split' from my host-birth personality. All are co-conscious, that is they share memories. While my principal alter, the youngest, a baby girl, is the most prominent in my psyche, there is no hierarchy or sub-systems within my psyche.

In DID terms, Dylan is both my birth and host personality. I have never felt the need or inclination for my birth personality to relinquish being my host personality. All my alters are pre-adolescent children who cannot negotiate the adult world unaided. Any suggestion of relinquishing my host personality to a child alter

The Adult Baby – An Identity on the Dissociation Spectrum
would feel psychologically unhealthy. I believe this is similar for most ABs. As Michael Bent explains, for ABs the adult self is the primary personality (the host in DID terms) and the baby or child persona is a sub-personality (alter in DID terms) (see *'The Identity Conflicts of the Adult Baby'* in the book *'Being an Adult Baby'* or in the article tab on the AB Discovery website).

Dax has a more complex set of relationships within his psyche. He has 9 alters. Starting with abuse at age seven there were successive waves of 'splits' as dissociation became the pattern for coping with trauma. The initial alters split directly from the host-birth personality. However, later, alters split from other alters. Christine Pattillo is another example of such a pattern. This has a bearing on which alters are co-conscious (although it is not the only factor). The fact that Dax's capacity to function in the external world is spread across alters also results in more complexity.

Dax is also not his system's 'birth' personality. Dax became the host personality by necessity and circumstance. His system's birth personality, bearing the burden of childhood wounds, grew tired and less able to act as host. The course of Dax's life and his relocations around the world have separated the birth personality from familiar places. In turn, after hectic years of travel and relocation, Dax has grown tired and is relinquishing more space to other, more energetic alters.

For people with DID, sometimes the host personality and the birth personality will be the same, other times not (as with Dax). Robert Oxnam discovered the host personality who had fronted his life and career for decades had taken over from his birth personality after high school. His healing involved his birth personality taking back the host role. Christine Pattillo gives a compelling account of grappling with the terrifying prospect her birth personality would relinquish the host role in her psyche to one of her alters.

For people without DID, like myself, it is confronting to hear of the birth personality withdrawing from being the host personality. It can seem like the death of identity. DID is a challenge to expand our conception of what the 'self' can mean for different people. Dr Ross explains -

The Adult Baby – An Identity on the Dissociation Spectrum

"Most people with DID have had the same host personality since childhood. Sometimes, though, a previous host got overwhelmed or tired and went away inside. Another alter personality then took over and became the host. The main point is that the host personality is not 'the person' – or the 'real person' – the host is just one of the alter personalities, whose job is to be out front most of the time."

This separation of the host personality and the birth personality is fortunately not applicable to the vast majority of ABs. It may be relevant in some rare examples. There are several published accounts written by the partners of ABs which describe a lifestyle where the AB's child self appears to be equal to, or more salient, than their adult self. The parallel with DID shows the birth personality relinquishing being the host is a serious psychological threshold. That is increased where an adult personality is potentially relinquishing being the host to a child alter. This is discussed in Chapter 11.

Psychological Function of Dissociation and Alters

I believe DID and being AB serve different psychological functions. Let me explain.

The term 'psychological function' sounds very rational. That's misleading. We are referring to the deepest parts of our identities which are formed in the unconscious. The unconscious logic can only be discovered many years after the initial trauma.

I have read a few on-line posts indicating there are some ABs who are also DID. There is no indication this overlapping population is a significant proportion of either identity. This suggests that dissociation and alters serve a different psychological function for people with DID, compared to ABs.

For Dax, DID is about survival at its most fundamental level – both physical and psychological. It was about surviving childhood abuse that threatened both his will to live, and his capacity to develop a functional self that could navigate the external world.

The Adult Baby – An Identity on the Dissociation Spectrum

Dax's adult alters provide essential capabilities that complement those of his host personality. For Dax DID was, and remains, a functional alternative to suicide. This is not being dramatic. The ISSTD's 2010 Guidelines state -

> *"Suicidal and/or self-injurious behaviors are exceptionally common among DID patients; studies have shown that 67% of dissociative disorders patients report a history of repeated suicide attempts and 42% report a history of self-harm ... "*

For me, being AB is about overcoming an inner emotional deadness. Compared to the life-and-death issues of DID that might sound unimportant. It isn't to me. The legacy of an emotionally austere childhood threatened to suck much of the joy, tenderness, and hope out of my life. All my alters are children, and my principal alter is a baby toddler girl. Those alters give my psyche access to the life-giving and life-affirming qualities cited above.

For me, being AB is a functional alternative to neurosis.

We can see this difference between the two identities in terms of their childhood attachment with their mother/primary caregiver. I suspect for people with DID, the depth of their childhood trauma, and the sense of betrayal by those who should have protected them, shattered their attachment with their mother/primary caregiver in their unconscious. In contrast, for ABs the lesser level of trauma, has broken rather than shattered their trust and attachment with their mother/primary caregiver. In turn, that leaves the AB with a compelling unconscious desire to revisit and repair that attachment.

To understand this we need to look at childhood attachments. We understand them based on the widely accepted and empirically-based Attachment Theory developed by the psychiatrist and psychotherapist John Bowlby. (For a discussion of Attachment Theory see my book *'The Adult Baby Identity – Healing Childhood Wounds'.*) A positive bond between a child and their mother/primary caregiver is called a secure attachment. It allows a child to grow up feeling secure, confident to explore their world and express themselves, and to trust themselves and others. A broken

113

bond is called an insecure attachment. It has a reverse, negative effect on a child's self-esteem and trust. Children with insecure attachments are more at risk of being traumatized by the 'ordinary catastrophes' of childhood. People with insecure attachments have lifetime issues with loneliness, a hunger for love, and distrust either of others or themselves.

Insecure childhood attachments are very common. Studies replicated across advanced western countries indicate around one-third of all children have an insecure attachment. An insecure attachment arises because a mother/primary caregiver is not sufficiently attuned to the needs of their baby or young child. That can happen for any number of common reasons – fatigue, anxiety, depression, lack of family modelling. An insecure attachment can also be caused by abuse or neglect.

Both people with DID and ABs have insecure childhood attachments. No surprise there. But I believe they have different types of those insecure attachments. ABs have either one of the two most common types – either

- minimizing their own emotional needs, reflecting a lack of trust in others (called an avoidant insecure attachment) or
- becoming clingy and demanding, reflecting a lack of trust in themselves (called an ambivalent insecure attachment).

However, people with DID have a third, much more damaged type of insecure attachment, labelled a disorganized attachment. They flip between the two other attachment types, alternating between a phobia for attachment (avoidant) and a phobia for detachment (ambivalent). A disorganized attachment is essentially a label for the seemingly capricious, alter-driven shifts in behaviours which derive from severe amnesiac dissociation.

Unlike people with DID, ABs revisit infancy and early childhood for emotional comfort and psychological safety. We are unconsciously revisiting the broken childhood attachment with our mother/primary caregiver (the psychological mechanism we use is

The Adult Baby – An Identity on the Dissociation Spectrum
discussed in Chapter 13). AB's child alters are an unconscious
attempt to get or regain our caregiver's love. This is described in my
book *'The Adult Baby Identity – Healing Childhood Wounds'* -

> *"The character of the child persona of each AB is unique, just
> as the adult selves of ABs are unique. Yet I suspect that there is
> important common ground in the characters of AB's child
> personas. They emerge in response to the brokenness of an
> insecure childhood attachment and childhood trauma. They
> are a response to the fact that ABs, as children, often felt
> unloved. And like all children who feel unloved, ABs felt it must
> have been their fault. They felt themselves to be unlovable.*
>
> *Our child persona is the antidote to feeling unlovable. Our
> subconscious created the most lovable child it could. I can best
> illustrate this from my own life. Chrissie emerged from a
> temporary traumatic separation from my mother when I was
> aged three or four. My baby sister and I were left in the care of
> strangers. My sister was picked up and comforted by but I
> don't remember being so comforted. Is it any wonder that my
> child persona is a baby toddler girl? In my eyes it was my baby
> toddler sister who got the love. As the elder male child, instead,
> I got expectations to be grown up beyond my years and felt
> ashamed for not meeting them. In my eyes, I wasn't picked up
> and comforted because I was an unlovable failure.*
>
> *Our child personas are a way of affirming to our wounded
> Inner Child that they are lovable. ..."*

> *"Dressing to feel authentic is very important. The more I dress
> in baby clothes that look, and more importantly, feel right for
> Chrissie the more I feel like a real baby girl. I sometimes say to
> my sceptical wife that an outfit or piece of Chrissie's clothing is
> 'cute' – more accurately Chrissie feels 'cute' wearing it. There's
> a world of meaning in that word. It means more than just nice
> or pretty. It means feeling like a loveable, adorable baby girl –
> a little princess. That is central to the 'primal drama' in my
> psyche – I can go back to a time when there should be a secure*

attachment between baby and mother. Being cute means (this time), I'll be loved and comforted and protected."

An essential difference between DID and AB is the former is an unconscious flight from catastrophic childhood trauma (typically abuse), while the latter is an unconscious attempt to revisit childhood trauma (probably not abuse) to change the outcome.

A Final Word on Differences

A key purpose of this book is to show the hitherto unrecognized similarity between DID and being AB. Both are on the dissociation spectrum. However, DID and being AB are not the same. Amnesia fragments the psyche of people with DID in a way that is not true for ABs. That fragmentation creates a deeper wound and is far more difficult to heal than the Jekyll and Hyde duality of ABs. An analogy would be to say there is a 'family relationship' between the two identities, but the differences make us first cousins rather than siblings.

DID represents an unconscious flight from catastrophic childhood trauma while being AB represents an unconscious attempt to revisit childhood trauma to change the outcome.

12. Alienation and Self Absorption

We have discussed alters, the key similarity between DID and AB, and we have looked at the major differences between Dax and myself.

Now we can return to look at other similarities between Dax and myself. They include alienation from self and others and self-absorption. Each of these is discussed below.

Alienation

For Dax and myself, alienation from both ourselves and others is a powerful part of our experience of life. It is a legacy of an insecure child attachment and childhood trauma. It is reinforced by having to live in the closet with a stigmatized personal identity. It can be overcome by healing and conscious effort, but it remains a stress point in our psyches which comes to the fore in adverse circumstances.

The alienation comes from childhood trauma. It is particularly the experience of 'aloneness' identified by psychiatrist Jeffrey Smith and discussed in Chapter 3. Childhood abuse is commonly perpetrated by a family member or someone known to the family. The abused child sometimes tells someone and is disbelieved. Or they don't tell because they are afraid they will not be believed, or because the abuser has threatened them or others. Abused children feel alone and often betrayed by adults who should have protected them from harm.

Dax captures how the sense of childhood betrayal lives on-

"This is true for us even today, although we are adults ourselves ... We may appear to be physically mature but ... our growth has been stunted and fragmented because of trauma and our intense loathing of all adults is very prevalent in the way we perceive the world. We start from the perspective of don't tell, don't trust anyone, and maybe with time gradually learn to trust and open up, although this has not got easier

with age. ... We crave kindness, love and stability, simple things but often far outside our reach or the capabilities of the adults around us to provide."

The trauma I experienced had these same elements of aloneness and broken trust, even though it was not abuse. For example, in my generation, you didn't complain to anyone about schoolyard bullying because you would be thought of as weak. A traumatized child's experience of aloneness and betrayal is the deepest wound and it is the hardest to heal. It leads to lifelong issues of alienation and mistrust of others.

But not all the wounds belong to the past. Our identities are stigmatized by the world at large. Of necessity, we have lived the great majority of our lives 'in the closet'. Public understanding of both DID and being AB is growing, but it is off a very low base. We know disclosure of the true nature of our identities to the great majority of our acquaintances, colleagues, friends or family would commonly result in shock, fear and rejection.

Those are issues faced by people with many different minority identities. Because of the hard-won victories of gay and lesbian liberation, much of society has come to accept many LGBTQ identities. Difference on the basis of sexual orientation has become accepted by many. We have learned to understand being gay or lesbian or bisexual is not a contradiction with, for example, being a truck driver, a nurse, a mother, a father, a sibling, a friend. But difference on the basis of multiple consciousness is still not accepted. And it will not be accepted for some time to come. And when people don't accept multiple consciousness they must adopt other pathological views of our identity – we are 'bad or mad'. People still experience our identities as an irreconcilable and unacceptable contradiction of our visible personas.

As with any closeted and stigmatized minority identity, Dax and myself internalized much of those negative views. We did not trust ourselves, we pathologised our non-conforming sense of self, blamed ourselves for it and felt ashamed. We have both moved on, but you can't completely let go of the baggage when you need to

118

remain closeted because of a genuine fear of detriment. We are both committed to changing the public misunderstanding of our identities. We share that goal with many others.

Alienation does not just apply to your sense of self. It applies to your relationships with others. The aloneness and betrayal that comes with an insecure childhood attachment and childhood trauma creates a deep mistrust of others. We are too quick to believe we are on our own in a dangerous and uncaring world. We doubt we can ever truly connect with anyone but our most loved partners. Dax sums up this alienation from others -

> *"we see alienation as a response to survival. As much as we want acceptance and support we also want to be left alone because trying to function in an adult world ignorant of our mental health issues is unfathomable."*

The cruel irony is alienation from others is a self-fulfilling perspective – the more alienated we feel, the more we cut ourselves off from others. I am conscious of the potential for a downward spiral. That can make me discount my resilience and feel more fragile than I really am. The alienation overlays and exacerbates the difficulties of coming to terms with living with alters.

But people with DID, and ABs, are not alone in facing alienation. And like everyone else, there is an onus on us to find our way beyond it, to seek and affirm a healthy relationship with ourselves and with others. Most of the alienation belongs to experiences in the distant past. We don't need to carry that baggage into our future. Therapy can help if it's needed.

Self Absorption

I believe people with alters have a propensity for self-absorption, and for self-centeredness and selfishness in their relations with partners. Anybody in distress or crisis is necessarily self-absorbed and self-centred. I am talking about people with DID, and ABs, in our everyday lives.

The Adult Baby – An Identity on the Dissociation Spectrum

The self-absorption is understandable. Our alters are as real to us as our host personalities. We are living with an internal community or family which can demand, and also entertain, our attention. That is particularly true of child alters. Their delights and play are a source of fun and entertainment. Their tantrums can preoccupy us. Christine Pattillo's autobiography provides a vivid picture of a mesmerizing, warm, vibrant and boisterous family life amongst her alters. Cameron West's alters include a gaggle of engaging children. The interior landscape inhabited by Robert Oxnam's alters is dramatically gothic and entertaining. In both positive and negative states our alters constantly pull our attention inwards to ourselves. As necessary or satisfying as that can be for us, it can be experienced very differently by those closest to us. At worst we can be moody and withdrawn, and even in better times, we can simply be self-absorbed and oblivious to the needs and feelings of our loved ones.

For those of us who are more emotionally inhibited and mistrusting of others, our alters can be celebrated as a source of self-sufficiency. Dax says -

> *"My alters are a comfort to me, they are my brothers, they have my back and they share the same goal of survival as me. Because we are many, there is little or no time/space to have others in our lives. It doesn't negate the desire for acceptance or having friends but the reality is that self-absorption is all-consuming."*

This can become a way of pushing others away. Herschel Walker attributes the breakdown of his marriage to this mistaken self-sufficiency.

I suspect people with identities based on alters can be self-centred and selfish in their close relationships. Our loving partners carry a burden of sensitivity, care and protection of a multiple that is not wholly reciprocated. We often fail to understand what being on the 'wrong' end of one to many relationships means. We take relating to one personality for granted. Our partner is relating to multiple personalities. That was still true even before we

120

recognized we were multiples. Our partners dealt with the moodiness, irritability, withdrawal and outright tantrums by our unrecognized alters. Being on the 'one' end of a one-to-many relationship can be hard work.

The extra mile that loving partners go is clear in Christine Pattillo's description of her marriage to her loving husband Christopher, of Cameron West's description of his wife Rikki, Robert Oxnam's portrayal of his wife Vishakha, and Olga Trujillo's description of her first husband David.

That asymmetry is exacerbated by the natural self-centredness of child alters. Like any biological children, they can be demanding, selfish and greedy. Rosalie Bent says *"little Ones can be vain, selfish and arrogant."* Like biological children, they have to be taught to build reciprocal relationships with others.

Wounded, unhealed alters can also have a survival mentality. One of Dax's alters describes it so –

"Our DID is all-consuming, you have to be selfish, and focused on self-preservation at all cost."

Unless we consciously seek to balance it out, we can take more of our partner's lives and energy than we give. Every human being has a capacity for self-centredness and selfishness. Our conscience is the measure of our honesty about this capacity. Those of us who have alters have a stronger propensity to be self-absorbed than most, and all too often that becomes a stronger propensity for selfishness. We need to be careful that consciousness of our unique identities does not become emotional entitlement. Everybody is unique. Everybody has hidden pain. We need to strive that bit harder to overcome our negative traits and ensure we give at least as much as we ask of those closest to us.

Summary

Alienation from self and from others, and a capacity for self-absorption and asymmetry in close relationships are traits common to both people with DID and ABs. We need to recognize those traits and respond to them positively or we risk making living with alters more difficult than it needs to be.

13. Are AB's Child Alters Real Children?

It is obvious AB's child alters are not real in a physical sense. But what about psychologically?

Many ABs experience their Little or child alter, as a psychological refuge from the stresses and strains of adulthood. When they become their Little, they see and experience themselves as inhabiting the headspace of a baby or young child which is soothing and tranquil.

So, via their child alter, do ABs have the psyches of biological babies or young children?

To answer these questions we need to look at both subjective reality, and objective reality. We'll start with subjective reality.

Subjective Reality

Alters are subjectively real.

That statement can seem condescending or pejorative – like the way you might characterise a child's imaginary friend. For adults, it can sound like an alter is an indulgence – perhaps of a weak mind.

That is not so.

Although our alters are later elaborated by our conscious minds, they originated in our sub-conscious when we were biological children. AB's involuntary triggering of the need for nappies, or the conflicts of the binge and purge cycle, are testament to that. Trauma rewired our psyches. We have lived all our adult life with that rewiring. Initially, with repression, our conscious mind may not even know we have alters. And when repression breaks down, our conscious minds can spend years or decades denying what our unconscious wants to foist on us. For example, I was horrified to realize my principal child alter, might be a girl. I fought accepting that for years.

We know how powerful the mind, especially the sub-conscious mind, can be in relation to the body. I refer in Chapter 4 to the way for some people with amnesic DID, switches between alters can manifest in changes in the physical body – shifts between being allergic and non-allergic, to medicines working and not working, to feeling pain and not feeling pain etc. Our psyche genuinely experiences our alters as real. They are more than metaphorical in the way singletons have an 'inner child'. This is not imagination or 'creative visualisation'.

Because they originate deep in the subconscious we know from DID dissociated alters cannot be wished or reasoned away. Removing alters as separate personalities, takes years of intensive psychotherapy to rewire the psyche (more on this in Chapter 14). Medication has little or no effect on dissociated trauma and alters (although it is sometimes used for associated symptoms like depression or anxiety).

Validation

There is a compelling validation that AB's child alters do replicate part of the psyche of a biological baby or very young child. The replication is in the way AB's gain a deep level of grounding and comfort from their nappies and other baby items. It is not an affectation. But how? Why is a soft or wet nappy so comforting? Why is a favourite soft toy so calming? Or favourite baby clothes? Or a pacifier? Or a bottle? After all a wet nappy or any of these things are not intrinsically comforting for most adults – most would find them annoying, if not downright discomforting. They ARE deeply comforting and calming for adult babies.

The answer is these objects provide comfort to the AB's child alter through exactly the same psychological mechanism as they do for biological babies and young children. It is commonly understood these objects serve as a substitute for the continuous presence of the mother/caregiver. That's why they help the child go to sleep or tolerate the temporary absence of the caregiver. They are called transitional objects.

The way they work in the psyche of the child was first understood by the renowned paediatrician and psychotherapist Donald Winnicott (see the references for citations). It is not just a case of a child deriving comfort from a familiar, but physically inanimate object. In the psyche of the child, it represents and embodies the caregiver – the object *is* the caregiver. It is called a transitional object because it exists between subjective and objective reality. The child's psyche endows an inanimate object with a subjective meaning which is not intrinsic in its objective, physical form. As transitional phenomena, the object's meaning goes beyond the confines of the child's mind, and is apparent to, and can be shared with, others. So a caregiver might ask a crying or fussing child, 'want your teddy,' knowing it has a special meaning for the child.

This psychological mechanism works at the deepest, earliest levels of a child's psyche. Biological children first create transitional objects when they are between 4 and 12 months old. That is before they have language or abstract thought. For ABs to gain such a deep level of comfort from childhood transitional objects means they must be replicating part of the psyche of a baby or young child. That is not something normal adults can access. I find that a compelling argument.

So now we understand why nappies are such a powerful part of being AB. The familiarity of nappies is a source of comfort for our child alters. But it's a lot more than that. Because the nappy is a transitional object, when we wear them, ABs are unconsciously recreating the presence of a loving caregiver. We are doing that because our child alter replicates *some* of the deepest parts of the psyche of a biological child. A wet nappy increases its efficacy as a transitional object. Presumably, that harkens back to the time when a wet nappy made the presence and attention of a caregiver more likely. That's why ABs find nappies so comforting.

Similarly when my baby alter Chrissie, hugs her favourite stuffed toys in bed they are not just cuddly but inanimate objects.

She really feels like they are friends protecting her – just like any small child feels.

When AB's accept their child alters, through the psychological power of transitional objects, we have access to this deep level of self-nurturing. That can comfort and heal our the insecure childhood attachment with our caregiver - if we pursue a psychologically healthy path (more on the latter in Chapter 15). It is important to remember that transitional objects are a means by which a child comforts *themselves*. They represent the child's first step towards psychological independence.

Objective Reality

So, from the above discussion, we might think ABs have the psyche of a biological child.

It is not so.

That's for two reasons. Firstly, our child alter exists in the same psyche as our adult host. Secondly, the Little or child headspace we visualize is an artificial construct of our adult psyche. Each of these points is discussed below.

Because ABs do not have amnesia, our child alter is co-conscious with our adult host. Each knows of the existence and capabilities of the other. Thus our child alter co-exists with our adult mind. We cannot unlearn what we know as adults about the trials and tribulations of human existence. Thus we are not truly innocent as children are. We cannot jettison our responsibility to do for ourselves and for those who need us, as best we can, without being self-indulgent and incurring realistic guilt. Thus we are not truly carefree as children are. A securely attached young biological child can feel completely safe in the arms of a protector they sincerely believe to be infallible, selfless, omnipotent and immortal. But we cannot truly re-experience that safety because as adults we know no protector is endowed with all these qualities.

Even if we had amnesia as do people with DID, replicating our biological infancy or early childhood would not be a safe refuge from our adult lives and selves. In reality, biological infancy and early childhood is not the tranquil psychological refuge AB's imagine it to be. Such a view is the artificial construct of our *adult* minds.

Arguably, the human psyche never faces more daunting challenges, including powerful fears and conflicts, than between the age of six months and three or four years old. Look at the dramatic changes in the physical and psychological capabilities in a child over these years. The psyche has to work incredibly hard to accommodate and drive those changes. These stages are beyond conscious recall, but we understand them through the work of child development experts like the psychotherapist Donald Winnicott (see my book *'The Adult Baby Identity – Healing Childhood Wounds'* for a description of the development of a child's psyche in the first year of life.) These stages of life are not the ones you would really want to go back to for a soothing calm respite.

So, the way we see or experience our child alters is not an objectively accurate facsimile of the psyche of a biological baby or child. Our child alters are a construct of our sub-conscious, later consciously elaborated. Rosalie Bent understands this. As well as being the partner of an AB she is the mother of four biological children and a grandmother. Writing for the partners of ABs she says -

> *"What is actually happening is that your partner has deep un-met needs and therefore constructs a pseudo-personality that can help meet these needs. The power of an intelligent and creative mind takes a set of behaviours and thinking patterns that are deeply separated from the usual adult patterns and then builds an age, name and pseudo-personality around these needs and behaviours. Thus a 'little one' is born."*

The 'artificial' nature of this construct is also evident in Rosalie's observation that ABs typically dress or behave as Littles in ways which combine elements from different developmental stages that would be unlikely to coexist at the same time in a real child. This applies to me and my baby girl alter, Chrissie. I have jackets and knitted bonnets that belong to a very young baby's layette, onesies and babysuits such as a crawling baby might wear, and two-piece pyjamas and dungarees you could see on a toddler. I visualize Chrissie being breast and bottle-fed, sleeping in a cot and playing in a playpen – behaviours which are probably most consistent with the 'crawler' stage. But I also visualize her feeding herself (messily), running around (unsteadily), playing with dolls and watching kids' TV shows, attributes which belong to an older age, toddler or beyond.

Psychiatrist Colin Ross puts the case that child alters do not replicate the psyches of biological children -

> *"Many child alters do not actually function at their alleged age level cognitively. They often understand long words, abstract concepts, and moral dilemmas in a way that would be rare for a normal child of that age. Others do seem to have a childish way of thinking. ...*
>
> *A scientific demonstration that child alters do not function cognitively at their alleged age would not invalidate DID. It would only prove that they are not real children. Such evidence, however, would challenge the overliteral view, according to which alters represent a concrete fixation in cognitive development. In my view, child alters are not packets of childness retained in a surrounding sea of adult psyche. They are stylized packets of adult psyche. ...*
>
> *The therapist shouldn't believe that child alters are really children, any more than he believes that demon alters are really demons, or that the patient is really possessed by her dead mother when an alter claims to be the mother. On the other hand, clinicians work within the patient's beliefs and worldview to a varying extent. The child alter personalities are always key components of the personality system in terms of the planning of therapy." [Dissociative Identity Disorder: Diagnosis, Clinical Features, and Treatment of Multiple Personality p147]*

The Adult Baby – An Identity on the Dissociation Spectrum

As Dr Ross indicates, there are many examples of alters in DID which we could never confuse with objective reality, even at a psychological level. Many people with DID who had been sexually abused as children by people in overtly religious contexts had alters who were demonic or satanic. Two of Robert Oxnam's original alters were a witch and a pair of disembodied eyes (reminiscent of Sauron in the fantasy Lord of the Rings). The uninformed might think of this as crazy. But we understand these alters as the psyche's response to childhood trauma; the child's psyche way of making sense of their experience. An AB's child alters belong to this broad phenomena of dissociated alters. We should not expect they replicate objectively real psychological states.

But I disagree with a key point made by Dr Ross. As per the previous discussion, I believe the child alters of ABs do replicate part of the psyche of biological babies and very young children. They do that through the mechanism of transitional objects. It is one of the deepest and earliest psychological mechanisms developed by biological children. We can see this most in the comfort ABs derive from their nappies and those other transitional objects (stuffed toys, pacifiers, bottles or whatever) which are most instinctual to them.

But beyond this deep subconscious mechanism, the rest of how AB's see and experience their child alters, is a construct of their adult psyches. That doesn't make it false or make-believe, but we should not confuse it with the psyche of biological children.

Summary

Because alters are not objectively real doesn't mean they are imaginary, an affectation, or the indulgence of a weak mind. They are deeply rooted in the subconscious and are compelling real to the person who has them. They cannot be willed, reasoned or medicated away.

ABs do not have the psyche of a biological child. Because we don't have amnesia, our child alter and our adult host are aware of each other's existence and capabilities. That means we cannot be truly innocent, or truly carefree, or feel as protected, as a biological baby or child. The way we visualize and experience our child alter is a construct of our adult psyches. But our child alter does replicate part of the psyche of a biological baby, specifically through the comfort we gain through transitional objects.

14. Are Alters Psychologically Healthy?

Okay, so we understand people with DID and ABs both have subjectively real alters.

But is having alters psychologically healthy?

Amongst the experts on dissociation and DID there are a range of views. The prevailing expert view is alters are a risk to psychological health. Other experts believe people can live safe and happy lives with alters. Both views emerged early in the development of the contemporary understanding of DID, and have persisted ever since. Each of these is discussed below.

Alters Are a Psychological Risk

The prevailing expert view is living with alters will always be a risk to psychological health. The strongly preferred outcome of the treatment of DID or OSDD is to fuse the alters back into a unitary psyche. I refer to this as the 'fusionist' view.

Psychiatrists Richard P Kluft and Colin A Ross are pioneers in the treatment of DID. From the 1980s and 1990s, they have been proponents of this adverse view of alters. It is reflected in the current (2010) version of the ISSTD's Guidelines. They state -

> *"R. P. Kluft (1993a) has argued that the most stable treatment outcome is final fusion—complete integration, merger, and loss of separateness—of all identity states. However, even after undergoing considerable treatment, a considerable number of DID patients will not be able to achieve final fusion and/or will not see fusion as desirable. Many factors can contribute to patients being unable to achieve final fusion: chronic and serious situational stress; avoidance of unresolved, extremely painful life issues, including traumatic memories; lack of financial resources for treatment; comorbid medical disorders; advanced age; significant unremitting DSM Axis I and/or Axis*

II comorbidities; and/or significant narcissistic investment in the alternate identities and/or DID itself; among others. Accordingly, a more realistic long-term outcome for some patients may be a cooperative arrangement sometimes called a "resolution"—that is, sufficiently integrated and coordinated functioning among alternate identities to promote optimal functioning. However, patients who achieve a cooperative arrangement rather than final fusion may be more vulnerable to later decompensation (into florid DID and/or PTSD) when sufficiently stressed."

For its' proponents, the idea of fusion is a positive one. The alters merge with the host and the positive capabilities and traits of the alters are not lost but become available to the whole psyche. Colin Ross in his book *'Dissociative Identity Disorder: Diagnosis, Clinical Features, and Treatment of Multiple Personality'* describes a 'fusion ritual' – mental imagery intended to reassure clients nothing positive is lost from their life as a 'multiple'. The damage and the pain held by the alters from the original trauma(s) is resolved in therapy before fusion, and is not carried forward. The person now has a unitary psyche. There are no 'fault lines' remaining in the psyche which might again fracture in the face of future stresses or crises. To effect fusion requires years of intensive weekly therapy to rewire the psyche.

The problem with this view of alters is not the idea of fusion. For some people with DID, moving to a unitary psyche may be a Godsend which relieves them of symptoms that have blighted their lives. There is nothing wrong with giving 'multiples' the option of fusion in therapy. The problem is the proponents of fusion stigmatise the other pathway to psychological health, cooperation between alters, in terms which are biased and harmful. Opposition or reluctance by a person with alters, to see them disappear, is stigmatized as psychological weakness or ill-health. The return of alters after their fusion into a unitary psyche is stigmatized and referred to as a 'relapse'.

This can be seen in several points in the description of Dr Kluft's views above. There is scant regard for a 'multiple' not choosing fusion. It is largely stigmatized as an inability or failure. In particular, attachment to alters is referred to as a possible example of a 'narcissistic investment in alternate identities'.

In a later passage, the ISSTD's 2010 Guidelines focus on 'narcissistic investment' as the sole reason why a multiple may not choose fusion –

> *"Fusion rituals are useful when, as a result of psychotherapeutic work, separateness no longer serves any meaningful function for the patient's intrapsychic and environmental adaptation. At this point, if the patient is no longer narcissistically invested in maintaining the particular separateness, fusion is ready to occur."*

In his recent (2018) book Dr Ross says –

> *"The goal of treatment for DID is stable integration – according to me. But that may not be the client's goal. Some people want to stop at the stage where all the parts are co-conscious and working together – this is their choice and it may be the right choice for them, and that's fine.*
>
> *Why do I think that integration is the best goal? For several reasons: (1) Why would you want to live with a little bit of mental disorder rather than none? (2) It takes less time and energy to be one person compared to managing a whole group inside. (3) Who knows how long the 'everybody in harmony' status will last? It seems that if you stop at the cooperating system stage, then life deals you severe trauma in the future, you are more likely to lapse back into conflicted, symptomatic DID – if you are integrated, this is less likely.*
>
> *There is no research literature comparing the long-term outcomes for fully integrated versus partially integrated DID. All opinions on the subject are opinions, not scientific facts – some opinions are educated, some are not.*
>
> *Reasons people give for not wanting to be fully integrated include: (1) I'll be lonely. (2) I'll miss them. (3) I don't want to*

get rid of them. (4) I'm functioning fine as I am. (5) I can't handle it on my own. Each of these reasons can be legitimate or just a form of denial and avoidance. It varies from case to case. The main thing is not to be dogmatic about integration, either pro or con." [Treatment of Dissociative Identity Disorder: Techniques and Strategies for Stabilisation]

Dr Ross's terms 'stable or full integration' is synonymous with Dr Kluft's term 'fusion'. Dr Ross makes clear he sees the continuing presence of alters as a risk. I characterise this as tolerating rather than accepting alters. However, he pays greater regard to the self-determination of people with alters, and 'owns' his views as (educated) personal opinion in the absence of clear research evidence backing either position.

This adverse view is reflected in the fusionist approach to alters in therapy. Even though fusionists recognize it is necessary to work with alters, the latter is still regarded as a risk to be contained. We can gain an idea of the nature of that risk from the following reference in the ISSTD's 2010 Guidelines -

"It is countertherapeutic to suggest that the patient create additional alternate identities, to name identities when they have no names (although the patient may choose names if he or she wishes), or to suggest that identities function in a more elaborated and autonomous way than they already are functioning."

This passage reflects an understandable concern to avoid either (a) the accusation the therapist is 'seeding' alters in the mind of a suggestable client or (b) exacerbating fragmentation in the psyches of distressed multiples. However, it refers pejoratively to the alters functioning in an 'elaborated' way. Presumably, this will then be an obstacle to a person agreeing to fuse their alters with the host – the 'narcissistic investment' referred to above.

The problem is this stigmatizes the cooperation option where multiples warmly embrace their alters. I suspect Olga Trujillo and Herschel Walker's distant and impersonal relationship with their alters reflects their psychiatrists' adverse, fusionist view. This

The Adult Baby – An Identity on the Dissociation Spectrum
runs counter to the usual trajectory discussed in Chapter 10 whereby the expression of alters grows and expands. Presumably, mental health professionals with this perspective would regard most ABs elaboration of the personality of their Little or child alter as psychologically unhealthy.

A recent (2016) text on dissociation for therapists, *'Treating Trauma Related Dissociation: A Practical Integrative Approach'*, refers to the re-emergence of alters after fusion as a 'relapse'. It discusses strategies for 'relapse prevention'. This makes it clear alters are seen as pathological.

This adverse view also extends to the interaction between a person's alters and their partner. The above text cites the following instruction -

> *"It is important for the partner not to call out parts other than the adult self of the patient, but to learn simple ground techniques that help the adult part of the patient to stay present and to return should there be a switch. Partners should not interact regularly with child or other parts of the patient, except to help the patient return to an adult and grounded place. This is essential because the more parts are active in daily life, the more autonomous they become, and significant relationship issues may be avoided by both parties by only dealing with more functional adult parts."* [Treating Trauma Related Dissociation: A Practical Integrative Approach]

From the perspective of the cooperative approach to alters, the above instruction is cruel and inhumane. It would preclude or stigmatise the warm accepting relationships between a person's alters and their partner described in earlier chapters. We have seen in several of the autobiographies these relationships were a positive turning point in the lives of people with DID. That was the case for Dax and myself. All of that healing would be prevented or undone by a therapist following the above text.

Presumably, this adverse view would also extend to any concrete recognition of Littles by partners. The ISSTD's Guidelines state –

> *"Reparenting" techniques such as sustained holding, simulated bottle or breastfeeding, and so on are clinically inappropriate and unduly regressive behaviours that fall below the current standard of care for any patient."*

Colin Ross explains in his book *'Dissociative Identity Disorder: Diagnosis, Clinical Features, and Treatment of Multiple Personality'* the simulated breastfeeding refers to that action by a therapist, rather than a partner. However it still clear that actions by either an AB or their partner which physically meet the needs of their Little or child alter (like wearing or changing nappies) would not be viewed positively.

This adverse view of alters places therapists in a difficult ethical position with their clients. Therapists are aware their view that alters should fuse back into a unitary psyche would not be well received by many of their clients. The ISSTD's Guidelines state -

> *"However, clinicians should not attempt to press for fusion before the patient is clinically ready for this. Premature attempts at fusion may cause significant distress for the DID patient or, alternatively, a superficial compliance wherein the alternate identities in question attempt to please the therapist by seeming to disappear."*

Therapists with an adverse view of alters seem to be placed in the difficult position of dissembling with their clients. They seem not to disclose their views about fusion in the first stages of therapy because that would be an obstacle to the trust and safety their clients need to feel for an effective therapeutic relationship.

Dr Smith says –

> *"When therapists are too enthusiastic about integration, patients tend to become suspicious of their motives. The decision of whether to integrate is best left to the patient."*

The Adult Baby – An Identity on the Dissociation Spectrum

Dr Smith's injunction to respect the choice of the patient is an ethically sound resolution of this difficult position. Dr Smith did exactly as he enjoins – his client, Robert Oxnam, chose to live happily with his three remaining alters.

Unfortunately, some therapists are so certain of their view about what is best for their clients, that dissembling shades into ethically doubtful intransigence. The 2016 text referred to above, coaches therapists on how to manipulate clients towards their hidden agenda of fusion -

> *"Once therapy has progressed to the point where the parts are working well together for the most part and at least some traumatic memories have been integrated, the therapist can begin to pique the patient's curiosity about fusion in an indirect way. **The therapist should regularly ask in a curious way,** I wonder what keeps those parts of you separate from you? Or, Have you ever thought about why those parts still need to be separate from each other? Have you ever thought about why that part of you has never grown up? I'm curious about what it might be like for you if those parts were closer together?"*

The three authors of this text are respected experts on dissociation. One, Kathy Steele, is the past (2008-9) President of the International Society for the Study of Trauma and Dissociation. Their certitude is reflected in the explicit endorsement of manipulative intransigence. There is scant space in this certitude to acknowledge there is no clear research evidence favouring fusion as an outcome, or to respect a client's choice there is a different way to psychological health (as per Colin Ross above).

Amongst therapists, there may be an association between this intransigent certitude about alters and an adherence to the more mechanistic therapist-driven schools of psychology. Those are schools such as Freudian psychoanalysis, or B.F. Skinner's Behaviourism and its derivatives; Learning Theory, Cognitive Behaviour Therapy (CBT) and Dialectical Behaviour Theory (DBT). The 2016 text cited above seems to be strongly influenced by DBT.

The Adult Baby – An Identity on the Dissociation Spectrum
These mechanistic theories can be contrasted with the greater respect for the client's self-determination in humanistic theories of psychology.

In fairness to the mental health professionals who hold an adverse view of alters, we need to understand many have spent decades working with clients for whom dissociative conditions are distressing, debilitating and life-threatening. These mental health professionals have in the last four decades contributed to a vast improvement in public and professional understanding of debilitating dissociation and its treatment. That being said, in my view, manipulative intransigence is therapeutically and ethically doubtful.

A Positive View of Alters

Fortunately, there are other experts and mental health professionals who have a positive view of alters. They believe it is psychologically healthy for alters to continue to exist as separate personalities, provided they work together as a team or a family. I refer to this as the 'cooperation' view.

One of the other pioneers in understanding dissociation, psychiatrist and paediatrician Frank W. Putnam, propounded this view in his 1989 text the *'Diagnosis and Treatment of Multiple Personality Disorders'*. This perspective has been recently restated by Psychiatrist David Yeung in his 2018 book -

> *"Although much of the writing on DID suggests that the goal of therapy is to integrate the alters into a unitary personality, that was never my goal. My approach is to help them become, as Putnam recommends, a fully functioning unit. If the alters are fused into one personality, there is a risk that without their main defence – dissociation – integrated patients may lack sufficient protection against the ordinary stresses of life, and thus be subject to splitting again in the future." [Engaging Multiple Personalities Volume 1: Contextual Case Histories]*

The cooperation option means the alters work as a team with the host. The extent of cooperation can vary. At one end of the scale, it can be sufficient for daily functioning although dysfunctions remain. Dax has this level of cooperation. Some of his alters are co-conscious, although most are not. There is little or no conflict between alters. Amnesia is still an issue and so is switching.

At the other end of the scale, full cooperation means the alters are like a family, each loving and respecting the others. There is no amnesia and all the alters are co-conscious. Shifting is more common than switching. The alters may be co-present. I fit this pattern. I suspect non-conflicted ABs would also fit this level of cooperation. Christine Pattillo, Cameron West and Robert Oxnam are examples of people with DID who have completed therapy and chosen to live with healed alters as an essential part of their personal identity.

This is the view in the self-help book 'Got Parts: An Insiders Guide to Managing Life Successfully with Dissociative Identity Disorder' which says –

> *"Parts are never going to disappear or go away; they will always be there, and part of you. Individual parts will always remain separately individual, but the goal of re-integration is to become aware of each other and working so seamlessly and cooperatively together, with shared information and regarding switches, that you can live and function in the outside world with a minimum of distress, without others, even knowing about your multiplicity unless you choose to disclose it."*

Dr Yeung's position has the ethical and therapeutic advantage that it does not require him to dissemble with his patients. He is not pursuing a hidden agenda which he knows is contrary to their wishes. As can be seen in his published case studies his position also allowed him to welcome an accepting relationship between a client's partner and the client's alters. This is a humane and therapeutic position, compared to the prohibition on such acceptance by proponents of fusion.

The Adult Baby – An Identity on the Dissociation Spectrum

Dr Yeung's comment that people who formerly had alters may be less resilient after fusion, is important to understand. People with alters have been living with multiple consciousness since they were young children, albeit this may have gone unrecognized until much later in life. Typically, their alters split within their psyche in childhood, before adolescence. Often they are in mid-life before they are correctly diagnosed. They have never lived with a unitary psyche as a teenager or an adult. Requiring a person who has lived with alters to transition to a unitary psyche is effectively a bold experiment. It is analogous to hitting the command 'restore factory settings' on a vintage laptop computer or PC which has decades of patches and upgrades, while hoping (with your fingers crossed) you can successfully load new, better software.

The 2016 text *'Treating Trauma Related Dissociation: A Practical Integrative Approach'* recognizes the significance of the change from multiple consciousness to a unitary psyche. It cites a range of difficulties the person may encounter. None of these are debilitating but they do suggest a decreased level of resilience, hopefully just for the short term. This underscores that pushing a 'multiple' to fusion is an experiment with that person's psyche. In this context the intransigent certitude and lack of humility of some of the therapists quoted above is disturbing.

Stigmatizing opposition by a multiple to fusion as a 'narcissistic investment in their alters' is the clearest example of this lack of humility. It disparages the psychologically healthy reasons for multiples to prefer accepting their alters as a team or family, over fusion into a unitary psyche.

Take me. My psyche split off alters between the ages of four and ten. I have been living with the behaviours driven by a child alter since I was ten. I am in my late fifties. I have never lived with a unitary psyche as an adult. Discovering I am a multiple helped me make sense of myself and my life in a deeper way. Making friends with my child alters has given me a sense of 'coming home' to myself. My whole psyche has access to their positive qualities. My girl child alter has helped me move beyond seeing things from a purely male perspective. My alters are a healing response to an insecure childhood attachment and its legacy; a life course shaped by the resulting emotionally inhibited, avoidant and anxious host personality. You cannot 'cure' an insecure childhood attachment, nor overthrow an entire life course. But you can find an internal source of warmth, safety and inspiration that enables you to better love yourself and others. My alters are a loving internal family. They overturn a lifetime fear of emptiness and loneliness. I am better, happier and more resilient for accepting them. I have fulfilled my obligations to society. I don't have anything to prove. I can be me. I am human, imperfect, but labelling all of that a narcissistic investment is inaccurate, arrogant and offensive.

AB's sexual fetish for nappies is also likely to be an obstacle to fusion. After adolescence the means by which we derive sexual pleasure is pretty hard-wired into our psyches, it's been reinforced many times by a powerful reward and isn't amenable to change. So even after fusion, our sexual fetish is going to keep pulling AB's back to the nappies which powerfully evokes our child alter.

I suspect many multiples will have their own sound reasons for choosing to continue to live with their alters. There are indications a significant proportion, probably the majority of people with DID in therapy do not want or effect fusion. The ISSTD's Guidelines state -

"Systematically collected outcome data from case series and treatment studies indicated that 16.7% to 33% of those DID patients achieved full integration (i.e., final fusion; Coons & Bowman, 2001; Coons & Sterne, 1986; Ellason & Ross, 1997)."

Remember that fusion takes years of intensive weekly psychotherapy. That is accessed by a tiny minority of the much larger population who have substantial dissociative symptoms. So stigmatizing the option for psychological health which is available to, and chosen by, most people with significant dissociation symptoms is harmful and counterproductive.

The cooperation approach is supported by a school of psychology named Internal Family Systems (IFS) therapy which has

The Adult Baby – An Identity on the Dissociation Spectrum
emerged since the 1980s. It is premised on the cooperative team approach. IFS is applicable to multiples with dissociated alters, and to singletons with metaphorical inner parts. It was developed by psychotherapist Richard Schwartz based on his work with bulimic clients. This may not be coincidental. I have read eating disorders may sometimes have their origin in dissociated trauma. For a discussion of IFS see my book *'The Adult Baby Identity – A Self Help Guide'* or search Amazon for books by Richard Schwartz or Jay Earley.

Dax, from the vantage point of reconciling DID with a functional and full life, says -

> *"There are risks attached to both perspectives [fusionist and cooperation]. The various approaches to therapy are constantly evolving and we learn more about the complexities of DID. The category of DDNOS didn't exist when I was diagnosed, it has evolved as more and more individuals are identified as having DID. As professionals continue to map and share the facts of cases we hope that patterns will emerge that can be supported by corrective therapy. Failure to understand the causes of trauma will ultimately result in more fragmentation and mental health suffering. A professional with a balanced approach, an open mind and a non-judgemental attitude will have a positive impact on the individuals they work with."*

> *"Treatment protocols only have merit when you truly understand the footprint of the individual. Trying to cookie cut a solution is not productive, and in the long term can cause more fragmentation. Positive support, guidance and clear communication are key factors inhaling someone with DID to understand their condition and its complexities."*

I believe these sentiments are valid for any multiple.

Identity

What the adverse, fusionist view of alters does not take into account is the issue of personal identity. Let me explain.

Remember, for a person to be diagnosed with DID they have to satisfy four criteria. The fourth criteria was –

The symptoms [listed in the other three criteria] cause clinically significant distress or impairment in social, occupational, or other important areas of functioning.

There is a similar criteria for Other Specified Dissociative Disorder (OSDD).

We have seen multiples who live with their alters as a cooperative team or a loving family can be free of distress or impairment. If there is no distress or impairment, the fourth diagnostic criteria above is not satisfied. The person satisfies the other criteria for DID or OSDD but there is no mental disorder. So what do you call it?

If a psychologically functional multiple chooses to live with alters it is a minority personal identity. They have a non-conforming sense of self. That makes it similar to, but not the same as LGBTQ identities. Transgender people are LGBTQ by virtue of having a compelling, non-conforming sense of self – they experience themselves as being of a different gender from the one they were born with. Having subjectively real alters is a non-conforming sense of self. That deserves the same respect and freedom from prejudice as LGBTQ identities.

It is not the place of the mental health professions to be the arbiter of minority personal identity. There is already a long dismal history of those professions causing harm to stigmatized minorities while being certain they were doing good. This includes stigmatizing gay and lesbian people as having a mental disorder, and stigmatizing transgender people as being fetishists or covert homosexuals. This harm is associated with unwavering certitude on the part of mental health professionals they knew what was good for their clients, disregarding and stigmatizing any contrary views by those same clients. The need of multiples in acute distress for guidance from mental health professionals does not validate a disregard for the personal experience and choices of the large population of people with significant dissociation.

The Nature of Identity

If we accept DID and being AB as identities on the dissociation spectrum, it prompts the question, how can a positive identity be borne from trauma?

The answer lies in understanding the nature of identity. For all of us, I believe the foundation of our identity is formed in the sub-conscious. That is different from the 'superstructure' of our identity, which we build in both our conscious and sub-conscious mind. We can come to understand why our identity has the foundation it does. We can make something positive of that foundation. But it is beyond our conscious mind to change those basic building blocks. I believe this is true for all, LGBTQ people and non-LGBTQ people.

The sub-conscious foundation of our identity, no matter how strange it may seem, represents our psyche's best solution to what our biology and our early environment bequeathed us. That foundation was our psyche's way of optimizing our chances for 'life, liberty and the pursuit of happiness', even in the face of factors which threatened to diminish or even destroy those chances. When we think about identities born from trauma, like being AB or DID, we need to remember they are the *responses* to difficult or pathogenic circumstances.

We should not judge such identities by the difficulties or trauma from which they arose, but rather by their success in creating a capacity for happiness and self-determination.

I owe this perspective to the psychotherapist Dr Michael Bader. In his book *'Arousal: the Secret Logic of Sexual Fantasies'* he takes the approach our sexual fantasies are our psyche's sub-conscious solution to finding sexual arousal and pleasure in the face

144

of pathogenic beliefs formed from our upbringing. Those pathogenic beliefs would otherwise destroy any capacity for sexual pleasure. No matter how strange our sexual fantasies they are perfectly comprehensible and serve a healthy function. I have extended this compelling and liberating logic to identity and happiness more generally.

Summary

There are conflicting expert views about whether living with alters is psychologically healthy. The 'fusionist' view is living with alters, even after therapy and self-acceptance, remains a psychological risk. Proponents of this view hold the definitive outcome is to fuse alters back into a unitary psyche. The positive traits and capabilities of alters become available to the whole psyche. The alternative, 'cooperation' view is multiples will be more resilient by living with their alters as a mutually supporting team or loving family. Both fusion and cooperation are valid options. It should be the choice of the multiple, not their therapist. Neither option should be stigmatized. I believe many ABs will favour the cooperation option. If a psychologically functional multiple chooses to live with alters it is a minority personal identity. That deserves the same respect and freedom from prejudice as LGBTQ identities.

.

15. The Challenges for ABs Living With Alters

ABs cannot be blind to the psychological challenges of living with our alters.

I disagree with the fusionist view of alters discussed in the last chapter. Even where a multiple can access and afford years of intensive psychotherapy, I believe many will be more resilient by choosing cooperation; to live with their alters as a team or family. But it would be unwise to dismiss the concerns of the experts about the risks of living with alters.

We have complex psyches. That brings both unique gifts and unique risks. Dax describes his alters as a 'two-edged sword'. We have seen that alters are dynamic. They are a source of change within our psyche. So it is not a case of reaching some endpoint and saying 'it's all okay now'. We need to periodically check if our path is taking us in the right direction.

As a multiple, I have learned to think of my psychological health in terms of my alters. If I'm out of balance, getting stressed, compulsive or obsessive, I ask myself 'what's up with my alters?' My wife will ask the same question. Often (not always) the source will one of my alters getting 'off beam'. Unfortunately, as multiples, sometimes we are only as 'together' as our most 'off' alter.

For multiples, psychological health means your alter(s) and your host are working well together. Each has a role to fulfil. Each respects the feelings, needs and role of the others. It's like a happy, psychologically healthy family. As a multiple, our psychological health reflects the state of our whole psyche, not just one personality. If one personality (either alter or host) is having everything their way, to the detriment of the other(s), then we are heading into trouble.

The Middle Road

I believe for ABs, living with alters in a psychologically healthy way, involves walking a middle road between pitfalls on either side.

The **first** pitfall is not accepting the subjective reality of our child alter(s).

The **second** pitfall is not accepting the objective reality that we are not biological children, either physically or psychologically.

Failure to accept either reality is psychologically unhealthy. Rosalie Bent describes this as the "all-important goal of balancing the need to be Little, with the real world requirement to be an adult."

Our child alters are subjectively real. They are more than metaphorical in the way singletons have an 'inner child'. They are a compelling presence in our psyche. A part of us really does think, feel, perceive, and at times act, like a young child (or rather our version of a young child). That got hard-wired in by trauma when we were biological children. Denying that reality twists our minds like a pretzel. It can make us neurotic. Denying the needs of that subjectively real child for nurture and safety leaves us feeling depleted in a way that cannot be salved by anything else.

Despite our child alters, in objective reality, we are not biological children, either physically or psychologically. Although we replicate *some* aspects we do not have the psyche of a biological child. While we can feel comforted and protected by nurturing our child alter, our adult minds and responsibilities cannot be jettisoned.

And in reality, biological infancy and early childhood is not the tranquil psychological refuge AB's imagine it to be. Such a view is the artificial construct of our *adult* minds. Our alters are a construct of our sub-conscious, later consciously elaborated. That doesn't make them fake. They hold fundamental components of our psyche we need to live whole lives. They can be a healthy part of our psyche. But we should not make the mistake of thinking they are a complete or accurate facsimile of the psyche of a biological child.

Challenges to Our Psychological Balance

So it's keeping on the middle road. How difficult can that be?

Sometimes it can be very difficult. As a multiple, we need to accept a subjective reality which contradicts objective reality. As a result, we live with two unwelcome but constant adjuncts to our identity – doubt and cognitive dissonance.

'Got Parts: An Insider's Guide to Managing Life Successfully with Dissociative Identity Disorder' tells us -

> *"There may be times when you may begin to wonder, or doubt whether your traumatic experience ever happened, or if it was really 'that bad'. There may also be times when you may question, even go into denial about whether or not you really are DID [AB]. This is very normal. ... Don't get stuck here, or let this de-rail you. ... Sometimes it comes down to intuition, faith, trust and deciding that even though you don't have all the answers, or don't know everything you long to know ... you can still move on in reclaiming your life."*

The doubt is about our sense of self. How can our AB identity be real when it is such a contradiction of our adult and visible selves? Is it just an over-active imagination? Are we crazy? We are the only ones who directly experience the child inside. We know we can never convince someone who chooses not to believe our subjective experience. To them, we are 'bad or mad'. Even after we accept ourselves, our doubt still lurks in the shadows. One of the cruel ironies of being AB, is before we accept ourselves we are afraid our child alter is real, and after we accept ourselves we are afraid they aren't.

Another key reason that ABs wear nappies, and all the rest, is to reassure ourselves our child alter is real – to bridge the chasm between our subjective reality, and visible, objective reality. The

149

nappies are a visible sign of a compelling sense of self which is otherwise invisible and unprovable.

Cognitive Dissonance

We also live with cognitive dissonance. The Wikipedia article of the same name defines that as –

> *"cognitive dissonance is the mental discomfort (psychological stress) experienced by a person who holds two or more contradictory beliefs, ideas, or values."*

For ABs, our cognitive dissonance comes from the contradiction between being functional adults who also experience ourselves as infants or young children. There is a stark disparity between how our child alter feels to us, and what we see when we look in the mirror. That is especially so for the estimated 50 per cent of male ABs who have a female Little. In my case, the hirsute older man dressed in 'baby drag' in the mirror can look grotesquely different from the cute adorable baby girl in my psyche. That difference is reinforced by most of our interactions with the world. Those interactions confirm only the existence of our adult host, to the exclusion of our child alter.

This cognitive dissonance can make us feel bad. Depending on what is going on for us, it can make us feel uncomfortable, or painful, or even tormented. If this seems overdramatic we need to consider several parallels that demonstrate the power of cognitive dissonance when it comes to personal identity. One is transgender people, another is people with anorexia.

Felix Conrad in his book *'How to Jedi Mind Trick Your Gender Dysphoria'* describes the pain some male-to-female transgender people experience when they realize, even if they fully transitioned and had gender reassignment surgery, they will never pass for a woman in a way that fulfils the self-image in their psyche. It can be tormenting. Failure to accept the cruel constraints of biology can become an obsession that takes over and blights their lives. (Though both dysphoria and cognitive dissonance are describing the same experience, I prefer the latter. Dysphoria is associated exclusively with transgender people and cognitive dissonance better describes what creates the discomfort or distress.)

People with anorexia have a cognitive distortion; when they look in the mirror they see a fat person that contradicts the trim self-image they have in their psyche. The cognitive dissonance between those two images is tormenting and drives their self-destructive behaviour. In this context, it is not too much of a stretch to compare being AB and anorexia. Psychiatrist Colin Ross describes DID and identity alteration (alters) as a cognitive distortion. I think the description is unkind, but accurate. I am not suggesting ABs are transgender or anorexic, rather pointing out the power of cognitive dissonance when it comes to personal identity.

It doesn't seem people with DID have the same struggle with cognitive dissonance as ABs. I believe this is because of the different psychological functions dissociation serves for the two identities (as discussed in Chapter 11). People with DID are not driven by the same unconscious need to revisit childhood as ABs.

The only long term, psychologically healthy answer to doubt and cognitive dissonance is self-acceptance – to accept our child alter is subjectively real, *but not* objectively real. Self-acceptance is learning to trust our experience of our self - to trust it even when we are struggling with ourself, or with life. Self-acceptance really does work: to the extent that we trust our subjective experience, we are fortified against doubt and cognitive dissonance. Self-acceptance is continual, slow-yielding, self-disciplined effort.

Denial of Subjective Reality

So, sometimes painful doubt and cognitive dissonance will cause us to veer off the middle road.

In the first half of our life course as ABs, before we accept ourselves, the culprit is most likely doubt. With few or no signposts to guide us, we doubt our experience of ourselves. *I'm an adult. How can I sometimes feel like a baby or very young child?* That leads us to deny the subjective reality of having a child alter. The problem in this stage is what psychiatrist Colin Ross calls 'host resistance' (discussed in Chapter 10). Our adult host identifies itself as "us", our psyche, to the exclusion of our child alter(s). They reject the existence of our child alter because they want to disavow the alter's needs, and the alter's origin in trauma and insecure attachment. Our adult host struggles to accept our alters are a real and valid part of our psyche. The worst form of host resistance is the savage rejection of our child alter in the purge part of the 'binge and purge' cycle.

We have two choices. We can deny and reject our child alter, or we can accept them and make what we want of our identity. For people with DID, and ABs, denial of our subjective reality is our enemy. It *will* screw us up. The way to psychological health is to accept and nurture our child alter, and to build a loving and harmonious relationship between our child alter and our adult host. Speaking from personal experience, I can say this is healing and transformative. That's the same route as for people with DID. Other books cover accepting child alters extensively so I will provide just a summary here.

Nurturing

Child alters are subjectively real. They have real needs. Imagine having a neglected or ignored small child in your household. Sooner, rather than later, they are going to get distressed or angry, or both, and they are going to let you know about it. If you're a person with DID, or you're AB, your child alter is no different.

Like biological children, child alters need to be nurtured on a daily basis and to feel protected. Every AB, and every child alter is unique. You need to work out what best nurtures your child alter. See Rosalie Bent's book *'There's Still A Baby in My Bed'* or my book *'The Adult Baby Identity – A Self Help Guide'* for useful thoughts on nurturing. Because child alters are subjectively real, they have access to the same deep sources of comfort as very young biological children. I'm talking about nappies, but also stuffed toys, a security blanket, or pacifiers or bottles.

Nurturing our child alters is self-love in the best sense of the term, and heals not just the child alter but the other alters as well. Providing nurturing turns angry, dysfunctional adult or adolescent alters from persecutors to protectors. They feel good about themselves and that removes the dysfunctions. This is true of both Dax and myself. The autobiographies of Christine Pattillo and Cameron West show how embracing and nurturing child alters can work for people with DID as well as it does for ABs.

Denial of Objective Reality

In the second half of our life course as ABs, the problem is usually cognitive dissonance. It goes like this: 'I have a compelling experience of sometimes feeling like a baby or very young child. But daily, my interactions with the world, keep telling me I'm 100% adult. It's painful having my feelings fight my mind'.

That leads us into toying with denying the objective reality that we are not biological children. I discuss this at greater length than the denial of subjective reality as it is not as widely covered elsewhere. It is the reverse of host resistance. It comes from our adult host growing tired and demoralized by cognitive dissonance and wanting to surrender that burden by giving way to our child alter.

It is an AB's adult host that struggles most with our identity of being a multiple with a child alter. Our child alter doesn't need to convince themselves they are real. They know they are. It is our adult host that bears the burden of cognitive dissonance. They are the alter who 'fronts' our psyche to the world. They are the alter that is most impacted by having to live with the fact that almost all of their daily interactions with others affirms only our adult side and denies the existence and need of our child alter(s). ABs alters are co-conscious and often co-present. So, our adult host is always aware of our child alter but they have to keep up the pretence to the rest of the world that the child alter doesn't exist. This can be cognitive dissonance at its worst. It can be exhausting and demoralizing.

From this place, it can seem like a solution for the adult host to step back, and cede more space in the psyche to the child alter.

Some ABs come to believe it is not their (adult host's) role to nurture and regulate the demands of their child alter, but their partner's. It's nice for our child alter(s) to have the love of the adult host's partner. A loving partner accepts the AB's child alter as subjectively real. The partner relates to the alter in some fashion as a caregiver. For some that will include changing nappies and bottle feeding or the like.

But our partner, no matter how accepting and loving, cannot supplant the role of the adult host in the psyche of the AB. Some ABs believe they can completely transfer this role as adult host to their partner. It represents trying to export the self-regulation and resilience of a healthy psyche to another person. That is incompatible with psychological health and stability.

Why? Because it denies the objective reality we do not have the psyche of a biological child. ABs do not have amnesia, our subjectively real child alter is co-conscious with our adult host. Each knows of the existence and capabilities of the other. Thus our child alter co-exists with our adult mind. A young child's psychological dependence on a parent is a necessary stage of their development. The same thing in an adult is unhealthy. That's for two reasons:

1. because a child's psyche is yet to gain adult capability, their dependence is not a denial of reality, indulgent or unhealthy; and

2. we do not share the child's sincere belief that our caregiver is infallible, selfless, omnipotent and immortal and thus can provide absolute safety for our psyche. As adults, we cannot unlearn the understanding that no caregiver can provide absolute safety, and we must be the first guarantor of our own psychological safety and well being. Others can add immeasurably to our sense of safety and well being

but they cannot substitute for the strength we must find within our psyche.

Remember too, that the deepest part of a child's psyche that is replicated by our child alters, transitional objects, represents a biological child comforting *themselves*. It is their first step beyond depending completely upon the nurturing of a primary caregiver. For an AB to read their child alter's need for transitional objects as consistent with their complete dependence on a partner's nurturing, is a misunderstanding of biological infancy.

The adult host ceding its space in our psyche to our child alter might seem like positive self-acceptance. It might seem like a kindness to our child alter. It is not so. For their child alter to feel safe and protected ABs need a strong adult host within their own psyche. In this, we are no different from other multiples. The DID self-help book *'Got Parts: An Insider's Guide to Managing Life Successfully With Dissociative Identity Disorder'*, describes this -

> *"Remember to love, to cherish, to value these young parts. ... It can take great patience, finesse and wisdom to deal with wounded 'littles' ... Yet, as they realise **the 'bigs' in the System [psyche] will keep them safe**, the rewards are well worth the investment of time and effort as they shed layers of fear and distrust and to learn to be open and loving and inquisitive and playful as they do their own healing work."*

The key point (bolded) in the quotation is that child alters need to be cared and protected, primarily, by the adult alters within the person's *own* psyche.

Only finding the strength within our psyche to care for our child alter is consistent with both our subjective *and* our objective reality. There is no sustainable safety for our child alter if our whole psyche renounces adult strength and resilience and is weak and vulnerable. It is impossible to remake ourselves into a biological child and trying to do so will cause us psychological harm. You can't be genuinely psychologically safe when you know you are consciously denying objective reality.

The Adult Baby – An Identity on the Dissociation Spectrum

That is a fraught road for anyone with an identity which originated in childhood dissociation. In the original childhood trauma, we lacked adult coping skills. Denying objective reality was a survival mechanism which detached us from adverse circumstances that threatened to overwhelm our psyche. It was a source of resilience. But unhealthy DID shows us continuing to rely on dissociation, into adulthood when we do have adult coping skills, becomes dysfunctional. The reality we don't want to acknowledge doesn't go away. Continued reliance on dissociation makes people less resilient and more vulnerable.

How do you know if you are veering off the middle road into denying objective reality? I believe this commonly manifests in two ways –

1. an unhealthy infatuation with fantasies of permanent regression; and
2. seeking to replicate the physical lifestyle of a biological child for the greater part of the day or even 24/7, and an unhealthy infatuation with the child alter supplanting the adult host.

Each of these is discussed below.

Fantasies of Permanent Regression

There is a vast stock of AB fiction on-line. One of the most common themes is permanent regression to infancy, whether voluntary or involuntary. The reach of this theme indicates this is a powerful idea for ABs.

Sometimes indulging fantasies of permanent regression is positive or harmless – a temporary respite from the lesser discomforts of cognitive dissonance, and the self-discipline involved in accepting our complex dual identity. But when we are in a bad place and stray off the middle road these fantasies are both a symptom and a cause of psychological malaise. I stress the difference between these fantasies being harmless or negative is the state of mind of the AB.

The Adult Baby – An Identity on the Dissociation Spectrum

When we are in a bad place, cognitive dissonance grows more burdensome. The temptation is to set aside the hard work of self-acceptance for a quick or easy fix. Then our use of AB fiction can become unhealthy. Fantasies of permanent regression can express and feed a desire to deny the objective reality that we are not biological children. It can get into our heads in a bad way.

ABs are a sub-DID group with a subjective identity derived from dissociation. For us, fantasy can be a particularly psycho-active ingredient. Let me explain. The ISSTD Guidelines describe people with DID as being 'highly hypnotizable'. This does not only refer to trances induced by a therapist. It also refers to the use of imagery and fantasy by multiples themselves. The ISSTD Guidelines state -

> *"... dissociative patients, usually unwittingly, use a variety of self-hypnotic strategies in an unbidden, uncontrolled, and disorganized way, and teaching them to exert some control over spontaneous hypnosis and self-hypnosis may allow them to contain certain distressing symptoms and to use their hypnotic talents to facilitate constructive self-care strategies."*

An example of the positive form of this self-hypnosis is using creative visualization to make a safe internal sanctuary for our alters, or nurture our child alter.

In the negative, it includes how off-balance ABs can become infatuated with fantasies of permanent regression. ABs can resort to these fantasies and the related on-line material frequently and compulsively. This is a powerful form of self-hypnosis as described in the Guidelines. That can lead to a negative trajectory. It can fetishize our identity as a multiple through an infatuation with B&D / power exchange themes. It can be reinforced by compulsive masturbation driven by painful cognitive dissonance (see the discussion in Chapter 16 about the relationship between cognitive dissonance and sexual climax). Eventually, that makes the cognitive dissonance and the doubt worse. In turn that feeds the need for more quick or easy fixes and a preoccupation with a 24/7 AB lifestyle.

The Adult Baby – An Identity on the Dissociation Spectrum

Sometimes, when doubt and cognitive dissonance are weighing us down and drawing us into fetish depictions of our identity or power exchange relationship models, we need a reality check. Conduct a thought experiment. Take any given circumstance or depiction, either from fantasy or from real life. Take the nappies and the AB themes out of the equation. Is that situation psychologically healthy or unhealthy? Nappies and AB themes are not a magic ingredient. If the situation would be unhealthy without them, adding them, doesn't make it healthy. There are no quick or easy alternatives to self-acceptance of our dual identity.

Given that ABs are susceptible to triggering, it would be helpful for AB fiction or true-life books to carry trigger warnings. The warning would list the key themes in the book ie. permanent regression, power exchange or B&D relationships etc. The warning would alert potential readers who had recently experienced shame, compulsive behaviours or obsessive thoughts in relation to being AB, to look after their self-care and delay reading the book until they were in a better place with their identity.

Replicating the Physical Lifestyle of a Biological Child

For some psychologically vulnerable ABs, the denial of our objective reality can lead to wanting to replicate more and more of the physical lifestyle of a biological infant or small child in a way that is detrimental to the healthy role of their adult host.

By this, I mean going beyond providing physical comfort for our child alter in a way that allows our adult host to have an equal share of our daily life. It's fine to wear nappies openly in private, wear nappies discretely in public, have a private room which is a child's bedroom or nursery or sleep at night as an infant or toddler. None of these stops our adult host being able to live an adult life (and be accepted by others as an adult).

But some ABs want to go beyond this. On-line there are hypnosis tapes that purport to assist an AB to become incontinent, or to adopt on a full-time basis, other infantile traits such as a need for pacifiers or bottles. In social media, it is not uncommon to read posts by an AB seeking to become incontinent 24/7. Others advocate for the public permission to live openly as a child and go out in public dressed and acting as a biological child.

These ABs are seeking to physically replicate the lifestyle of a biological child. It represents an attempt to validate a reality that is subjective, to avoid painful doubt and cognitive dissonance. For psychologically vulnerable ABs this is a dangerous road to take. This is emphasized in the ISSTD Guidelines -

> *"In addition to being highly hypnotizable, some DID patients have been thought to be highly fantasy prone .... A minority may be so, although several studies suggest that most DID patients are only moderately fantasy prone ... Nonetheless, there is concern that at least some DID patients are vulnerable to confusing fantasy with authentic memory and/or mistaking experiences within the inner worlds of the personalities for events in external reality whether or not hypnosis is induced ..."*

I suspect the Guidelines are concerned with avoiding 'false' memories of childhood abuse. But for ABs the concern about multiples being fantasy-prone includes an obsession with the 24/7 AB lifestyle (which is based on an artificial 'fantasy' view of childhood).

Remember, being AB is an unconscious attempt to revisit childhood trauma and effect a different outcome – a secure attachment with a caregiver. We can make our peace with that. But when that becomes a flight from adulthood it becomes unhealthy.

It represents the adult host wanting to cede its proper place in the psyche to the child alter, and perhaps to cede the healthy self-regulation of their own psyche to a partner. We know from the above discussion, it is because the adult host has grown exhausted and demoralized by the constant burden of cognitive dissonance. In the extreme, this parallels situations where someone with DID changes their host personality. That is a major psychological threshold. For someone with DID, a child alter supplanting an adult personality as the host would be a grave indication of psychological

159

deterioration. It is no different for ABs. It is a denial of the objective reality ABs are not biological children, either physically or psychologically.

This is akin to the obsession Felix Conrad indicates can blight the lives of some transgender people. It is akin to the self-destructiveness of anorexia. For ABs, it represents the renunciation of adult resilience and surrender to self-absorption. One of the problems in going down this road is that an AB or their partner may believe they are in conscious control of the trajectory when they are not. They are using dissociation as a coping strategy. We know from DID, the real driver of that trajectory is repressed or denied childhood trauma. Good things don't drive trajectories that undermine our adult resilience and make us more psychologically vulnerable. Denying objective reality hits a fault line in our psyche as a multiple. Pursue that denial too hard, for too long and there is an escalating risk to psychological health. In a previous chapter, I quoted Dax saying he knew of people who failed to come to terms with being a multiple and it consumed them.

Understanding that ABs are multiples with a child alter which originated in childhood trauma means there is help for AB's struggling with this situation. Psychotherapy with a skilled psychotherapist, based on an accurate diagnosis of dissociation, offers the prospect of healthy relief and healing for a struggling AB and their demoralized and exhausted adult host. See appendix 2 for thoughts on finding the right therapist and psychotherapy.

What's Real?

Sometimes living with our dual identity can feel like living in a no-man's land betwixt subjective and objective reality. Sometimes we can lose track of what's real.

So what is real?

Our dual identity is real.

The need to balance the needs of both our adult and child alters is real.

The Adult Baby – An Identity on the Dissociation Spectrum

Our broken childhood attachment is real. If it wasn't, you wouldn't need nappies.

The childhood trauma is real. If it wasn't, you wouldn't have a Little/child alter.

I believe, like DID, being AB is a childhood-onset post-traumatic developmental disorder.

You didn't ask for any of it. It's not your fault. But you got it. You need to make your own peace with it.

The broken attachment and the trauma can be healed. You can't 'cure' either of them away, but you can make your peace with them.

Summary

For ABs, our child alters can be a gift. They give us access to innocent happiness and contentment which approaches that of a securely attached biological child. But as multiples, our psyches are complex and there are risks if we do not find a way to live safely with that complexity. We have to walk a middle road between denying the subjective reality of having child alters with their own needs, and denying the objective reality we are not biological children, either physically or psychologically.

As a result of our complex psyches, we cannot completely escape living with doubt and cognitive dissonance. They are sometimes painful. We are not the only minority identity with that challenge – for example, people who identify as transgender but chose not to transition, are in a similar boat. The only psychologically safe sustainable antidote to doubt and cognitive dissonance is acceptance of our dual subjective child/objective adult reality. Self-acceptance is a long, slow, self-disciplined effort. But it works. It does fortify you against doubt and cognitive dissonance. You can love and enjoy your child alter without having to prove they are objectively real.

The Adult Baby – An Identity on the Dissociation Spectrum

16. Alters and AB Sexuality

I am an unlikely person to be writing about sexuality. I am inhibited and strongly introverted. These are not the best qualifications for writing about this topic. But it's important and it's a big part of being AB. It contributes a great deal to the confusion and shame that conflicted ABs feel about their identity. And I believe that I have found insights that might help others to better understand themselves.

Most of what I understand about AB sexuality is based on my own experience. In the introduction, I said take what is helpful from this book, and leave the rest behind. That applies doubly to this chapter.

From what I have read in online forums and AB non-fiction books, I believe that my experience conforms with many other male ABs. However, there is comparatively little written from the perspective of female ABs, particularly when it comes to sexuality. So I don't know how similar or different this issue is for female ABs. For example, do they suffer, in the conflicted stage of our identity, from the same compulsive masturbation as male ABs? I don't know. There is a clear need for more writing from the perspective of female ABs.

For ABs, sex can be complicated. That's for three reasons –

1. we have a sexual fetish;
2. sex can involve a lot of involuntary switching between alters; and
3. the erotic 'target' of an AB's sexual fantasies may not be sex with a partner, but their own fantasised transformation into an adorable dependent baby.

Each of these is discussed below.

Fetish

Many mental health professionals and laypeople consider that being AB is a sexual fetish. That is how it is defined in the DSM.

The Adult Baby – An Identity on the Dissociation Spectrum

That's wrong in as much as the fetish for nappies/diapers is a *symptom* of being AB, not the cause. We are ABs because we have a subjectively real child alter, which dissociated in childhood trauma. But we still have a sexual fetish for nappies. Why? How?

The key is understanding the sequence of developments. I believe what came first was the broken (insecure) attachment with our mothers/primary caregivers. Remember, attachment patterns are established very early in life. They are well developed by the time a child is 12 months old. The insecure attachment made us more vulnerable to being traumatized by the 'ordinary catastrophes' of childhood, such as temporary separations from mother. The traumatic event or events came next. It was probably when we were still very young. In my case, the first traumatic event was when I was three or four years old. That's when our psyche first split off a child alter.

It seems for many ABs, the first experimentation and compulsion to wear nappies didn't manifest until some years later. Around the age of ten seems to be a common experience. For some it was much younger, even going back to age five or six. Whatever the exact age, it was before puberty. The nappies started off being a source of emotional comfort-driven from our subconscious by the needs of our unrecognized child alter.

Then along comes puberty and our adolescent host develops sexual needs and the beginnings of their sexual identity. This is grafted onto the existing most powerful dynamic in our psyche – our child alter. Voila! Nappy/diaper fetish. Nappies now serve two needs – our child alter's need for comfort and nurturing, and our adolescent host's sexual needs. Nappies are both a transitional object and a fetish object. And as we don't know we are multiples, these different needs are experienced as a tormenting conflict within ourselves.

How we derive sexual pleasure gets hard-wired pretty early in adolescence. Thereafter, the constant reinforcement of pleasure means those preferences aren't amenable to change. So even after we have accepted our identities as ABs, and as multiples, we will still have a nappy fetish. For me, nappies and fantasies of being babied are indispensable to sexual pleasure. The compulsive masturbation is gone, but the nappy fetish remains. I believe that would be true for ABs generally.

Switching and Sex

Sex is the circumstance most associated with involuntary and unrecognized switching between my alters. Switching commonly occurred in sexual arousal, and again immediately after sexual climax. That means in a short space of time three different alters were in executive control of my body. There was the alter before sexual arousal, a different one during sexual arousal and climax, and a third one after climax. When I was conflicted about being AB the switching was abrupt and brought confronting changes in my emotions and thoughts.

Take the example of the involuntary triggering of the need to put on a nappy. My experience is described below -

> *"I wanted nappies because they met a deep need within me. I wanted to enjoy the wonderful feeling of freedom, of coming home to myself, that wearing a nappy represented. I was often stressed, tense and anxious. The prospect of wearing a nappy promised at least a brief respite of being able to lose my adult worries and feel comforted and safe. But that goal always got hijacked with me becoming sexually aroused, and masturbating while wearing the nappy. A powerful climax was pretty much always guaranteed. But immediately after I would be filled with feelings of shame and remorse. I would hurriedly fling the nappy aside, put on my adult clothes and quickly tidy everything out of sight. The goal of being comforted in a really deep and satisfying way always seemed to be just out of reach."* ['The Adult Baby Identity - A Self Help Guide']

My reading suggests this is a fairly typical experience of male ABs. We can look again at this situation with our understanding of ABs being multiples. It was my child alter coming 'out' and desperate for nurturing and the comforting familiarity of a nappy that triggered my need to put on a nappy. But that purely emotional need didn't hold sway for long because nappies are a sexual fetish for my adult host. They needed the release of masturbation as an antidote to stress, anxiety and also to the conflicts about being AB in the first place. So, as the fetishized nappy caused sexual arousal, my adult host switched 'out' replacing my child alter in executive control.

Then, immediately after climax, my punitive parent alter switched out. They were angry and scared at the loss of control caused by the needs of my child alter and adult host. It was the revulsion of my punitive parent alter that caused me to immediately throw off the nappy and rush to 'tidy away' all the evidence of my AB side. No wonder masturbation was so compulsive and emotionally convulsive! Of course, before I accepted I was a multiple I didn't recognize this switching for what it was – I just lived with the abrupt and confronting shifts between emotional states.

Rosalie Bent describes the switching which occurs after sexual climax –

> *"One problem that may occur is known as the 'crash'. Orgasm usually causes the Little One to temporarily disappear and for the adult to re-emerge. In masturbation, this is expected and understood and is normally, relatively gentle. During sexual intercourse, however, the feelings and emotions are far more intense and can cause the re-emergence to be powerful, fast and at times, overwhelming. Be aware of it and comfort your adult if this happens. It is also a good reminder for both of you to realise that sex was actually between two adults, but the 'crash' can also sometimes be disturbing. Be prepared for tears at times. It is all worth it, however. The recovery from the crash is usually quick and becomes easier if the Little One is permitted to crash and then recover with you there, as his primary support."*

The Adult Baby – An Identity on the Dissociation Spectrum

Now that I have fully accepted myself as an AB and a multiple, it works a bit differently. Thankfully! My child alter gets to wear nappies at regular times each day. Most days that doesn't result in any inclination for my adult host to masturbate. On the occasions that I do masturbate, when I start to think about sexual fantasies that precede sexual arousal, my child alter switches inside. It is my adult host which enjoys the fetishized fantasies and reaches sexual climax. Afterwards, it is my child alter which switches back out to resume the comforting feelings of being in a nappy and have a nap. My punitive parent alter plays no part (I think with self-acceptance and retirement, they have either become dormant or fused with my adult host). The switching is not abrupt, more like shifting, without the conflicting emotions and needs.

Understanding all this has let me see that sex and specifically, fetishized sex, is driven by the needs of my adult host, not my child alter. As a result, I believe that AB's child alters seek only emotional comfort from wearing nappies.

The Erotic Target

That brings us to the third point above, the erotic target of an AB's sexual fantasies. What do I mean by erotic target? It is what fulfils your sexual fantasy, the endpoint that brings you to sexual climax. In researching this book it was a revelation to me to realise that the erotic target of my sexual fantasies was not sex with a partner. It was imagining myself to be an adorable, helpless and dependent baby. A desirable adult woman was always part of my sexual fantasies. But I realized that they are there as caregivers, not sexual partners. In my fantasies, they are treating me as a baby, not as a sexual object.

I owe this understanding to Felix Conrad's insight into transgender erotic fantasies. In his book 'Transgender: Fact or Fetish' he indicated that the erotic target of at least some male to female transgender people was not sex with a partner, but imagining themselves with the body of the woman that met the idealized self-image in their psyche. I realized this applied to me, except as an AB, I wasn't imagining myself as a woman, but as an adorable baby girl.

Sexual fantasies are notoriously individual and diverse. Perhaps this was just my 'thing' and had no relevance to other ABs? But then I looked at the erotic AB fiction I liked to read. All of it was based on stories where the protagonist was psychologically or physically turned into a helpless dependent baby. Depending on the story, the women characters may have played a sexual role, but that was ancillary. Their main role was to 'baby' the protagonist, not to relate to him as a sexual adult. Most of the detail elaborated in these stories is not about sex, but about how the male protagonist's adulthood is stripped away and how that makes him feel, willingly or unwillingly, like a baby. That's where the author's and the reader's attention lies. That was the erotic target, not sex with a partner.

There are a lot of these stories on-line which meant there was a market for them. It wasn't just me! I'm not saying this is the only game in town when it comes to AB sexual fantasies and AB fiction. But it does look like it's a sizeable part of the market, and hence a sizeable part of the AB population.

But how does this erotic target fit with an AB's alters? As we have seen, it is the adult host who is 'out' in an AB's sexual arousal and climax, not their child alter. Why does our adult host need sexual fantasies where they are transformed into an adorable baby? Because as we saw in the previous chapter, it is an AB's adult host that bears the burden of the sometimes painful cognitive dissonance about being AB. The fantasy and the erotic target salves that burden. At the point of climax, our adult host's identification with the child alter is complete and the painful cognitive dissonance is momentarily dispelled. For that brief moment, we are not a multiple. We are just our child alter. And we are adored – loved and protected – so that the broken childhood attachment is also repaired. That's why the need for masturbation is so compulsive and powerful for conflicted ABs. All this logic happens in our sub-conscious so most aren't aware of it.

I found corroboration of my experience in an account by Maggie Joyce. She is the partner of an AB, and the mother of her husband's Little, a baby girl named Melissa who identifies as a nine-month-old. Maggie provides the following account of her AB partner's sexual climax -

> *"The truly fascinating and possibly freaky aspect of this is that at the point of orgasm, she is as young as ever I see her. I can only imagine the psychological processes at work, but as she approaches orgasm, I can see in her face a lowering of her age until at that point, she is perhaps as close to a new-born as she gets. It only takes a few moments for her to return to her nine-month-old age again, but for a moment, she is new-born."*
> *['The Full Time Permanent Adult Infant']*

I believe Maggie is describing the point where the adult host is completely identified with the child alter. The rapid transition back to reality after sexual climax also helps us better understand the 'crash' earlier described by Rosalie Bent.

But what about all the fetish bondage and discipline (B&D) and power exchange themes in AB fiction? Doesn't that contradict the idea that our erotic target is not about sex? No. Those themes are what our adult host needs to bridge the chasm between what they believe sex should be about (sex with a partner), and the real erotic target of seeing ourselves an adorable helpless baby. Remember the phenomena of host resistance identified by psychiatrist Colin Ross and discussed in Chapter 10. Our adult host struggles to accept that our child alter is an equally real and valid part of our psyche. This is especially true of sex. A healthy child alter does not have an interest in sex. Sex is the province and need of our adult host or alters. But the deepest need of our adult host is to dispel the pain of cognitive dissonance. And that leaves a chasm between what our adult host believes sex should be about and what it's really about when you're an AB. That's where the fetish, B&D and power exchange themes come in.

In an earlier chapter, I mentioned psychotherapist Michael Bader's insightful understanding of the role of sexual fantasies. No matter how strange they may seem, our sexual fantasies allow us to find sexual pleasure in the face of pathogenic beliefs that we derived from our upbringing – beliefs that would otherwise prevent us from reaching sexual arousal and climax. For example, for someone who enjoys the submissive role in B&D, the fantasies are an antidote to our childhood fears that we are unimportant to our loved ones. If we could not counter this unconscious belief it would be impossible to gain sexual pleasure. Who could get sexually aroused either with a real partner or in fantasy, if we really believed that we are insignificant and undeserving of attention? The intense attention and focus of a 'dominant' in B&D fantasies is a reassurance that we do matter to them, we are important – loved. Again, this logic happens in our subconscious and most are unaware of it.

ABs have a broken childhood bond with our primary caregiver. A young child unconsciously takes responsibility for the broken bond because it is too terrifying to see a deficit in the caregiver upon whom they are completely dependent. So, unconsciously, the child believes the broken bond must be their fault. They are unloveable.

So an AB faces two major obstacles within their own psyche to sexual pleasure. Firstly, sex is an adult need and means sex with an adult partner, but the deepest need is release from the painful cognitive dissonance of the contradiction of simultaneously being both adult and child. Secondly, we have an unconscious belief that we are unloveable – we were unloveable as children, we are still unloveable as adults.

As Michael Bader says, fetish and B&D fantasies are the solutions to these obstacles. Typically the fantasies start with the protagonist being an adult. That's the starting point our adult host needs to feel okay about sex as an adult activity. Typically, (but not always) the fantasies involve the protagonist with someone who is, or has the prospect of being, a desirable sexual partner. Another tick for our adult host. The fantasy involves the 'partner' progressively transforming the protagonist into a submissive, dependent, infantilized figure. The protagonist may be willing, but is typically unwilling, with some ineffectual show of resistance. Unwilling submission is a sop to our punitive parent alter that we do not want what we really want, to surrender being an adult and the cognitive dissonance that goes with it.

As the fantasy progresses, the partner figure asserts their dominance. They effectively transform into a parent/caregiver substitute for the emerging unified adult-child figure. In some fantasies, the parent/caregiver may have had this character from the outset. In this situation, the unconscious mind converts B&D themes of dominance to signals the emerging baby of the fantasy is adored and safe. This works for both the adult host and the child alter. The eventual submission of the infantilized protagonist to the 'partner'/substitute parent-caregiver represents the adult host surrendering the burden of cognitive dissonance, of maintaining the pretence that the psyche is wholly adult. That goes to our adult host's deepest but unacknowledged need. Fetish discipline stands for unconditional parental love and devoted parental attention. For the child alter, this dispels the wound of the broken childhood attachment – they are loved and protected.

When we are conflicted about being AB, our resort to these fantasies is guilty and compulsive. We need their unconscious logic to reach sexual arousal and climax but we don't understand much of it. The conflict between our adult host and our child alter can be savage. That can drive us compulsively to the release of sexual climax and ever more extreme fantasies. Typically the B&D themes grow stronger with a greater degree of coercion, humiliation and punishment. That is intrinsically unhealthy. It can represent us punishing ourselves for the existence and real needs of our child alter. And the stronger B&D themes intensify our guilt. It can develop into a negative spiral. The circuit brake is that we exhaust ourselves sexually, physically. But it can still leave us in a dark place at the bottom of the spiral.

After we have genuinely accepted our child alter the absence of the conflict within our psyche drains the energy from compulsive sexual activity. The compulsion disappears. The nappy fetish remains. But the fantasies are less extreme. They still involve submission to a parent/caregiver substitute and some parental like discipline but it doesn't have the hard edge of coercion and humiliation. I believe that when fetish and B&D themes still play a large part in an AB's fantasies or in their self-image, it is a sign of still unresolved conflict about their identity as ABs.

Child Alters and Sex

That brings us to the issue of child alters and sex.

Obviously, people with DID, who may have child alters, have sex with their adult partners. However, the accounts I have read indicate psychologically healthy people with DID take great care not to involve their child alters in sexual activity. Once it is accepted that child alters are subjectively real, it could not be otherwise.

What about ABs? On-line, many ABs seem to have or seek DDLG (Dominant Daddy / Little Girl) relationships – or the gender converse, variously identified as Dominant Mummy or Caregiver / Little Boy, or similar. These relationships commonly include sexual relations and are generally thought of as a fetish, kink, or form of B&D. In these situations, the child self may appear to be involved in sexual activity. In a healthy situation, I believe that is not so.

As we have seen above, sex is the province and the need of an AB's adult host. An AB's child alter wants nappies (only) because they bring emotional comfort and safety. The sexual fetish dimension of nappies and power exchange practices belong to the adult host. In my experience, in sexual activity, my adult host self displaces my child alters.

This does not deny that DDLG or similar relationships can meet the emotional needs of child alters. The DDLG or equivalent relationship pattern can be seen as a potentially positive acceptance of a person's subjective reality of a child alter by their partner. For many people, it is probably the only available model of a relationship which can encompass the needs of imperfectly understood child alters.

However, I believe there are psychological risks in such relationships where there is not an understanding of dissociation and alters. The existence of unidentified and unhealed childhood trauma create a risk of psychological harm where sexual and power exchange behaviours do not respect the boundaries between the adult host and child alters.

A willingness by a multiple to involve their subjectively real child alter in sexual activity may be an indicator of sexual abuse in childhood. The psychiatrists familiar with DID indicate sometimes unhealed dysfunctional alters seek to replicate the abusive and exploitative relationships that caused the original childhood trauma. This can be based on a variety of dysfunctional motivations: an alter that loves the abuser, a desire to confirm the alter is bad and seek punishment or abasement, and so on. These motivations are unconscious but the repetition of the original abusive or and exploitive pattern reinforces the original trauma.

The boundary against involving a child alter in sexual activity must be upheld. The child alter is subjectively real. The same need to protect them (and the whole psyche) from psychological harm applies as for a biological child.

Summary

Sex is complicated for ABs! We have a sexual fetish for nappies. Our alters can switch several times before and after sex. And the erotic target of our sexual fantasies may not be sex with an adult partner, but our transformation into an adorable baby.

The Adult Baby – An Identity on the Dissociation Spectrum

17. Self Care for ABs

Self-care for ABs extends beyond the inside of our psyches.

We have the example of people with DID to know living with alters can be challenging. Everyone, whether they are singletons or multiples, needs to feel psychologically safe. But for multiples, it is a little more complicated. Alters are there 24/7. *Each* of them processes and sometimes reacts to the stimuli taken in by our senses. *Each* of them needs to feel safe and at ease, for us to go about our lives without disruption.

So self care, and the right self care, is essential. I believe that includes the following –

- a safe physical personal environment;
- a place of sanctuary within our psyche;
- to recognize our need for acceptance by loved ones;
- to recognize our need for fellowship with others like us;
- to have outlets for service and creativity;
- to be cautious about disclosure; and
- to come to terms with childhood trauma.

Each of these is discussed below.

Safe Physical Environment

Everybody needs a safe physical environment. Why that's important is a bit different for people living with alters.

ABs commonly need a somewhat sequestered environment that provides privacy because they have to conceal their lifestyle. The privacy conceals the wearing of nappies and baby clothes, and perhaps baby play. It also commonly conceals a large stock of baby clothes and paraphernalia. But I realized my need for a sequestered environment is not just about physical concealment of an AB lifestyle. Dax, with DID, has a similar need for a controllable environment, and his need has little to do with hiding a lifestyle.

The need relates to living with alters 24/7. It is a need for respite, to minimize stimuli which might trigger alters. Such stimuli include unpredictable interactions with others who are unaware or unaccepting of our alters. Speaking for his 'system' Dax says -

> *"We crave silence always, limit access to TV and rarely listen to music because, noise destroys our ability to focus and hear our thoughts. We like to hear the muffled sounds of each other. We are collectively more balanced and switching is controlled when interactions with people are limited."*

It is also a need not to have to hide - a freedom for alters to be out and express themselves and their needs without fear and inhibition.

A physical environment which meets these needs removes the apprehensions and uncertainty that replicate the symptoms of anxiety. Such an environment remains safe only when it's shared with a partner or others who understand and accept our alters. The form such a safe physical environment takes can vary. At its least, it is likely to involve a room where you can close the door on the outside. At its best, it's a whole dwelling, or even better, a dwelling in a surrounding physical space.

Dax's instinctive affinity for small islands makes perfect sense in this context. His preference is *'the smaller and more isolated the better'*. He explained islands represent safety because in a metaphorical sense they are circles – if you get lost you will end up safely back where you started. Cameron West lives with his wife in a house by the beach. Olga Trujillo lives on a small farm.

Internal sanctuary

A safe physical environment where alters don't have to hide and don't face uncontrolled and unpredictable interactions with others provides a place of respite to re-charge. But if you've got alters you can't live as a hermit. You have to be able to carry a place of psychological safety with you wherever you go.

For Dax and myself, a place of sanctuary within the psyche is very important. Dax describes it as the place where "we [his alters] take our thoughts in times of heightened anxiety and stress. It's a place without walls, it involves water, a never-ending horizon, peace and no people." Again, you can hear the echo of Dax's affinity for small islands in his conception of his internal sanctuary.

Having this internal sanctuary is a technique which is commonly recommended for people with DID. *'Got Parts: An Insiders Guide to Managing Life Successfully with Dissociative Identity Disorder'* says –

> *"Everyone in the System [psyche] needs to work together to create a safe space inside where you all reside. This place is sometimes known as the 'Dome'. This is where parts are when they are not 'out', and is a place to get to know each other better, and to do your healing work individually and together. ... Using the creative power of your imaginations, you invent this actual place inside you. It is very important to create the Dome together, and that it is safe. ... [it] can take any physical configuration ... Examples include a Sphere, or Pyramid, or Lighthouse, or Cathedral, or Log Cabin, or Tepee, or Space Station. It could be a beautiful place in nature, like a serene ocean shoreline or wildflower prairie or lush rainforest ..."*

Christine Pattillo describes and even provides a map of the internal share house where her alters and host personality reside when they aren't 'out'. Cameron West has an internal 'comfort room' for his alters.

I have an internal sanctuary. It is described in my book *'The Adult Baby Identity – A Self Help Guide'* -

> *My safe space is a country cottage. It is peaceful but not isolated. The house has a beautiful nursery with white wooden furniture, including a cot, changing table, and nursing chair; and is decorated in pink and soft pastel colours. There are*

windows and French doors opening onto a broad shady veranda. Beyond is a soft, soft lawn enclosed in a sturdy white open post fence that keeps wandering toddlers safe inside and everything else outside. ... In the day it is always barmy, not hot, and at nights it is cuddly cool – perfect for fuzzy, footed sleepers or pyjamas. It is lovely to visit when I am in bed falling sleep. It is where I take Chrissie if she gets frightened.

I suspect many ABs imagine a fully decked out nursery in their minds. Those who are fortunate to create a nursery in real life are transposing something that already exists in their imaginations.

Acceptance By Loved Ones

I believe ABs and people with DID share a fundamental need - to be believed about our subjective sense of self. Our subjective reality is compelling and fundamental to who we are. But we can't prove it to someone who doubts us. Being believed is an act of empathy which allows us to stop pretending about who we are around others. It lifts the heavy burden of hiding ourselves, and the awful fear of rejection.

For any multiple, once someone accepts our alters are subjectively real, they 'get' us – all our otherwise inexplicable traits and behaviours are completely understandable. (Accepting our subjective reality doesn't compel our loved ones to do anything – they have the same choices as we do in terms of how best to respond to this reality in a way that works for them.)

For ABs, the loving acceptance of a partner also soothes the cognitive dissonance we discussed above. It is powerful because it is an acceptance that is lived out every day, in small unconscious ways. It becomes normal and natural for you and your partner to feel you share your household with a young child.

One of the most challenging situations is for ABs who begin to accept their identities later in life, and who have an established marriage or partnership. There is an awful tension between not wanting to injure or lose a relationship with a beloved and admired life partner, but needing to be true to ourselves and not having to hide a fundamental part of our identity.

As ABs, we know the process of accepting ourselves wasn't easy or fast. Even with the best will of all involved, gaining the acceptance of loved ones, isn't likely to be any different. I suspect most ABs make lots of mistakes in seeking our partner's acceptance – initially we are too desperate and demanding. Compared to our own inner journey we expect our partner to fast track their own processes. We want to dictate what form our partner's acceptance of our subjective reality takes instead of allowing them to choose what is safe for them.

In the hiccups of that process or worst case if we are rejected, we can slip back into shame and denial. In seeking acceptance we can be clumsy and demanding. But we should never reproach ourselves for our need for acceptance. It's normal and healthy.

Fellowship With Like Others

Another important need is for the fellowship of those who share our identity.

The common experience of people with DID and ABs is we are adept at hiding in plain sight. With the prospect of real detriment from broad disclosure, we have to. But if we hide all the time from everyone, that is a road to neurosis. It is not psychologically healthy to go around experiencing ourselves as being the sole outlier in the human experience. No matter how introverted we may be, (like myself) our species are social animals. With that psychology hard-wired in our brains, outlier equals outcast, and outcasts don't live long and happy lives. We need the fellowship of others whose own identity validates ours.

As challenging as it may be, I don't believe there is a tenable longer-term alternative to reaching out to others like ourselves. I am in the early part of this journey so I am not well placed to add much further value on the topic. What I have discovered is, as imperfect as they are, online and social media environments, do provide opportunities for fellowship for those with rare, and misunderstood personal identities.

Service and Creativity

For Dax and myself, service to others in our working life offsets the alienation of having an identity the world doesn't accept. I suspect this is common to many people with minority personal identities. Dax is a gifted teacher for children with learning difficulties. He talks about his lifelong connection to children as a *'strong desire to nurture other children to make them stronger, smarter and less vulnerable than we were.'* I am proud of a career of service to the public good. For both of us, those vocations let us feel good about ourselves – in seeking to be of service to others, we weren't negatively defined by our misunderstood personal identities.

Having an outlet for our personal creativity has also helped us live with our challenging identities. Again, I suspect this is common to many people beyond those with DID, or ABs. Dax is at home in the digital world where his affinity with different media gives him a creative outlet. It is the basis for a successful online consultancy. He relates that success to his DID – which facilitated being able to learn and fulfil a range of roles such as website designer, tech support, service provider, content creator, and more. My creative outlet is writing. To me, writing seems especially suited to exploring and understanding identity, in fiction and non-fiction.

Outlets for service and creativity are important to everyone. They are particularly important for people who feel alienated because of their non-conforming personal identities.

Be Cautious In Disclosure

While accepting our need for the acceptance of our loved ones, and the fellowship of those like us, we also need to recognize general disclosure carries a strong risk of detriment.

The Adult Baby – An Identity on the Dissociation Spectrum

Some brave or fortunate multiples do live openly with their identity. Christine Pattillo and Robert Oxnam are examples. Most of us live 'in the closet' because we have a valid fear of harm from the prejudice and misconceptions of others. There are many occupations and employers where your job and your career would be at grave risk if your identity as a multiple were known. Robert Oxnam seems to have had to leave his former career as an international academic when he was 'outed' with DID.

Multiple consciousness scares people. It is equated with dangerous insanity and debilitating dysfunction. That's wrong. It's changing, but slowly. Even when people know multiple consciousness isn't a physical threat, it makes them feel unsafe. It represents the unknown. It is a departure from a unitary view of the psyche whose simplicity is comforting and safe.

I suspect most people are aware their own psyches are anything but simple – consciousness is multi-layered and at times contradictory. But denial is everywhere and it works. The notion of a simple, unitary psyche holds unwelcome questions at bay. Let's face it, if you have DID, or you are AB, we ultimately had to accept our less-than-straight-forward psyches because we had no choice. Other people don't want their option of denial taken away.

Psychiatrist Colin Ross provides the following advice to people with DID who ask 'Should I tell other people about my trauma and dissociation?' –

> "It really depends. Having a person who understands you is important and helpful. However, there are risks. For instance, the person may not understand, may not believe in what you say, may criticize you, may use this to attack you, or may tell this to others even without your permission. It is necessary to think carefully before you make the decision."

> "Another issue that comes up frequently is how much to tell other people about both your trauma and dissociation. Again, it is possible to err in both directions. If you tell too many people too many details too fast, you can drive people away. This isn't proof that you are unloveable. Cancer patients often

experience the same thing – many of their 'friends' can't cope with the cancer and disappear. This is when you learn who your true friends are. It's a painful process, but you end up with a smaller collection of true friends who you can focus on."

"For children, overall, the less they are told about your trauma and dissociation, the better. Certainly, you shouldn't explain trauma and dissociation to children under 10."

"For employers, generally, the less they know the better. Sometimes they need to be filled in for leave, disability or other reasons. It's probably better to say you have PTSD, anxiety or depression than to share a DID or OSDD diagnosis. That sets off fewer alarm bells in the outside system. Not telling all the details does not equal lying. It's your business, not theirs. Don't get pressured into telling more than you want to tell."

For ABs, the fear that some people will conflate our identity with paedophilia is a further risk in disclosure. There has been some progress in public understanding that this is not so, but the risk is still present.

The discussion above applies to simply advising others you are AB /OSDD. That's different from sharing the lifestyle of your very young child alter, their needs and behaviour with others. I believe that is a private matter to be shared only with carefully chosen loved ones. As ABs, we sometimes struggle with doubt and cognitive dissonance about our baby or child alters, even though they are compellingly real to us. It is asking too much of others to deal with that cognitive dissonance. The vast majority will not deal with it well, and will not thank us for asking them to make the attempt. You can't blame them for that.

But I do believe in working towards positive changes in public understanding so ABs can declare without detriment they are 'multiples', functional adults with a young child alter(s).

The Adult Baby – An Identity on the Dissociation Spectrum

Come to Terms With Past Trauma

I believe at the source of being AB there is dissociated childhood trauma, together with an insecure childhood attachment. If you have a 'Little' you are a multiple. A Little is an alter. The clear view of contemporary psychology is the source of alters is most likely childhood trauma. It isn't as devastating as that which caused DID, but it's still not good. Just as I believe denial can fuck us up, so can unacknowledged trauma.

Unhealed dissociated childhood trauma is an ongoing risk to our mental health. It predisposes you to anxiety and depression. It subtly warps your perceptions, most notably about yourself, in ways you do not see. It sneaks harmful baggage into the relationships with those you love – baggage you are not fully aware of, but your loved ones most likely are. It can lead you to toy with denying the objective reality you are not a biological child, either physically or psychologically.

Denial is the natural first response to the awareness there might be something bad at the back of the cupboard in our psyche. Don't let it be your last response. Don't be afraid of what is within your psyche. You are already living with it. The choice is between bumping around in the dark or turning on a light to see what needs to be healed. For ABs, dissociated trauma can be healed and that is life-changing. But it needs the help of skilled counsellor. See the appendix 2 on therapy for ABs as an identity on the dissociation spectrum.

Summary

Good self-care is essential for everybody. Living with alters puts a different 'spin' on what good self-care means for a multiple. Good self-care is the difference between living with alters as a gift, and living with alters as a blight.

18. Conclusion

At the start of the book, I talked about how each AB comes to feel their psyche is hard wired differently from those around them.

Well, now we can see it's true. Our psyches were rewired by trauma in our childhood. Dissociation gave us subjectively real child alters. The trauma and the alters were largely repressed in our subconscious for many years.

But not completely, even early on. As biological children, ABs had issues with their continence – toilet training or bedwetting. Years later, the regression to that fixation is the initial point where the repression of our child alter in our subconscious breaks down. Even though the existence of the child alter is at first not understood, they are the source of our craving to wear nappies. The feel of a nappy is a familiar source of comfort to them.

Our daydreams and fantasies are filled with images of being treated like dependent helpless babies and children. Over time, the 'acting out' of our child alter typically expands to other familiar sources of infantile comfort: stuffed toys, pacifiers, child or baby style clothing etcetera. These are a clear signal from our subconscious that we share our psyche with a small child. But typically it takes us many years to accept the blindingly obvious. We can't blame ourselves for that. We were taught to think of alters and multiple consciousness as indications of insanity. We weren't insane, so it must be something else. A fetish? A kink? Those were never good explanations, but they were the distraction our denial required.

But now we understand dissociation. Every person on the dissociation spectrum has a unique 'footprint'. Each different 'footprint' produces a unique experience of self and life. We can recognize DID and being AB are identities on the dissociation spectrum. DID is at the further end of the spectrum, while being AB is 'next door'. With a lifetime of sometimes compulsive infantile behaviours at odds with our adult selves, I believe being AB fits the category of OSDD – *Other Specified Dissociative Disorder*. In the absence of clinically significant distress or impairment, both DID and being AB are minority personal identities, not disorders.

The compelling similarity between DID and being AB is both have subjectively real alters which influence thought, feelings, perceptions and behaviour. For both, alters are present 24/7 and can potentially be triggered at any time. There are striking similarities in the description of child alters between people with DID and ABs.

But DID and being AB are not the same. The defining characteristic of DID is the combination of identity alteration and amnesia. The amnesia causes a devastating fragmentation of the psyche. Being AB is identity alteration without the amnesia. DID represents an unconscious flight from childhood trauma, while being AB is an unconscious attempt to revisit it to change the outcome. There is a family 'likeness' between DID and being AB - but with the important differences, we are like first cousins rather than siblings.

The presence or absence of amnesia produces a different experience of alters between the two identities. For many people with DID, switching means a distinct change between the host personality and an alter, or between alters. Even with co-consciousness, shared memory, if one is 'out', the others are in the background.

It's different for ABs. Typically their host adult personality and their child alter are co-present. That's a term used by Colin Ross, a psychiatrist and authority on trauma and dissociation. When the two are co-present they share the sensations and control over the body. That produces an experience of self which is more like shared consciousness. The change in focus between the host personality and alter is more like 'shifting' than 'switching'. We don't hear distinct voices or dialogue in our heads. It is a more subtle form of alters, consistent with OSDD. That is a key reason why being AB has not been correctly understood by mental health professionals and by ABs themselves.

The Adult Baby – An Identity on the Dissociation Spectrum

Okay, we understand being AB is an identity on the dissociation spectrum and we have one or more child alters.

So what now?

It boils down to four things –

1. accept your dual nature;
2. practice good self-care as a multiple;
3. be proud of who you are; and
4. see the gift in who you are.

Each of these is discussed below.

Accept Your Dual Nature

For ABs, denial of *either* our subjective reality, or objective reality, will mess us up. We have a child alter. It is not metaphorical like the inner child of a singleton. A part of our minds *really* does think, feel, perceive and sometimes act like a young child. Through our child alter we have access to innocent joy and contentment, and a feeling of being safe and protected, that most adult singletons don't. They can't be deeply comforted and settled like we can by a soft or wet nappy, or hugging or sleeping with a favourite soft toy. Our child alter's need to be nurtured is real, and must be met for us to live happily. But we are not biological children, either physically or psychologically. We are also adults.

But our dual nature can also be difficult to live with. It brings self-doubt and cognitive dissonance. The latter comes from the contradiction between the real child in our psyche and the visible, objectively real adult we see in the mirror, and experience in our interactions with the outside world.

The doubt and cognitive dissonance can sometimes be painful or tormenting. It can cause us to want to downplay or reject our dual nature in favour of one that embraces just the child. That leads us to flirt in ways that are psychologically unsafe with fantasies of permanent regression and notions of a full-time lifestyle as a child. There is no solution there. Going down that road

189

eventually only makes the cognitive dissonance worse. Taken to an extreme it creates dangerous psychological risks.

To be psychologically healthy, we need to accept our dual nature. Self-acceptance is long, slow, self-disciplined effort. But it does work. It fortifies us against doubt and cognitive dissonance. When we learn to trust the child in our psyche is REAL, we aren't tormented by trying to validate they are objectively real like a biological child.

Good Self Care

We are multiples. The example of people with DID shows us we need to practice good self-care to live happily and safely. As discussed in the last chapter that includes –

- a safe physical personal environment;
- a place of sanctuary within our psyche;
- to recognize our need for acceptance by loved ones;
- to recognize our need for fellowship with others like us;
- to have outlets for service and creativity;
- to be cautious about disclosure; and
- to come to terms with childhood trauma.

Be Proud

As ABs, I believe we are right to be proud of our identity. We can tread the road people of other minority identities have already trodden – from shame to pride.

DID or being AB can be incomprehensible to others. For a time in our lives, our own identities were incomprehensible to us. It is too, too easy to equate different with bad - especially unconsciously.

We cannot judge non-conforming identities by the difficulties or trauma from which they arose, but rather by their success in overcoming those challenges. Those identities can best be understood as the psyche's way of optimizing the chances for 'life, liberty and the pursuit of happiness', even in the face of factors in a person's early life which threatened to diminish or even destroy those chances. Understand the challenges and you will understand the identity. Once you accept the childhood trauma, and the subjective reality of alters, DID and being AB is completely understandable.

ABs show great courage in accepting our child alters, and not turning away from their genuine need for nurturing despite the unconventional way that need presents itself. We have kept faith with our inner child and our true self in the face of persistent public misunderstanding. Many ills of the world would be cured if there was a more general recognition we all have an inner child, and the need for nurturing is a universal need.

I believe just as ABs can learn much from people with DID, ABs also have something to show people with DID. That is the importance of child alters. For any multiple, I believe child alters are central to their healing and their happiness.

See the Gift

There is a gift in being a multiple – whether DID or AB. And that is understanding everyone's life is shaped by their unique subjective reality.

For almost everyone, there will be times in their life when the world does not understand or accept their subjective reality, and that causes pain and alienation. For example, a stranger cannot see we may be in deep grief, yet it shapes our experience of ourselves and life on an hourly and daily basis. In these circumstances, we can all feel very alone.

For all of us, understanding and accepting another's subjective reality about themselves even when that reality seems confronting or incomprehensible is an act of empathy, kindness and love.

The Adult Baby – An Identity on the Dissociation Spectrum

People with a non-conforming sense of self are well placed to understand this universal human experience. That is one of the reasons why society as a whole is better for accepting difference. It allows all, to better ask for and receive, the understanding of our own unique experience of ourselves.

Psychiatrist David Yeung says –

"There indeed people with DID who have healed. ... They do good things in the world and have the capacity to display great empathy towards others." [Engaging Multiple Personalities Volume 3]

Felix Conrad reached a similar view about the gift in being transgender. He says –

"we must forge our own meaning as to why we are the way we are. For me, that meaning lies in the fact that our ever-shifting minds give us an incredible reserve of empathy and understanding for others. That is like a super power. My advice is that you start mining that reserve ... and use your super power to change the world." [Quantum Desire: A Sexological Analysis of Crossdreaming]

I am proud Dax and I are giving that advice, our best shot. I know there are many, many others, either with DID, or who are ABs, who are doing the same.

Appendix 1 – Two Magnetic Resonance Imaging (MRI) Studies of DID

The two studies cited below use MRI to compare the brain structures of people with DID, sub-DID DDNOS, and 'healthy' people.

'Hippocampal and Amygdalar Volumes in Dissociative Identity Disorder' American Journal of Psychiatry. 2006 Apr; 163(4): 630–636. Vermetten, Eric; Schmahl, Christian; Lindner, Sanneke; Loewenstein, Richard J; Bremner, Douglas J.

'Volume of discrete brain structures in complex dissociative disorders: preliminary findings' in Progress in Brain Research, Vol. 167, 2008. Ehling, T; Nijenhius, E.R.S.; Krikke, A.P

The two articles are succinct, readily comprehensible to the lay reader and available free on-line (see the references). Both have useful lists of further references.

The two studies are summarized below.

2006 Study

The study covered 15 patients with a history of severe DID, and 23 healthy subjects without a psychiatric disorder, in Baltimore USA. The DID patients had a history of childhood abuse and had also been diagnosed with PTSD and major depression (both are commonly co-morbid with DID). They had a mean age of 42 years and an average of 16 years of education. All participating subjects were female (this may reflect an intention to remove the issue of age differences in the volume of the hippocampus from the study - unlike men there is no evidence the volume decreases with age in women aged 20 to 50).

Key points –

- Indicates it is the first study to demonstrate differences in key brain structures in people with DID.
- Of prior research, it states – " … essentially nothing is known about the neurobiology of dissociative identity disorder."
- Hippocampal volume was 19.2% smaller and amygdalar volume was 31.6% smaller in the patients with DID, compared to the healthy subjects.
- Indicates for this area of research generally, it is unclear whether smaller hippocampal volume is caused by trauma, or whether people born with smaller volume are more vulnerable to trauma and dissociation.
- Cites as the key implication of the study – "an understanding of dissociative identity disorder as a trauma-related disorder that involves neural circuitry alterations in brain areas associated with memory that are also affected in PTSD ..".

2008 Study

The study covered 10 DID-patients, 13 DDNOS-patients, 10 DID-patients who completely recovered from DID after lengthy psychotherapy (average duration 4.5 years), and 20 healthy controls. The study was conducted in the Netherlands. All participants were female.

Key points -

- Unlike the 2006 study, this one included a sub-DID DDNOS-1 group. People with DDNOS-1 have either well-developed identity alteration or significant amnesia, but not both (otherwise they would be DID). It is not clear if the people in this group had amnesia (unlike ABs) or identity alteration (like ABs).
- Unlike the 2006 study, this one also measured the volume of the parahippocampal gyrus (PHG) which

serves as an interface between the hippocampus and neocortex, and the amygdala.

- Hippocampus volume was 25% smaller in the patients with DID, compared to the healthy subjects.
- Patients with DDNOS were midway between those with DID and the healthy subjects, with 13-14% less hippocampus volume than the latter.
- Otherwise, the DID and DDNOS populations were similar, with both having 19-20% less PHG volume and 10-12% less amygdala volume, than the healthy control group.
- If the two groups with DID are compared, the recovered group had 9 – 18% (left & right respectively) more volume in the hippocampus, but not more PHG volume.
- Hippocampus and PHG volume were also strongly correlated with reported exposure to potentially traumatizing events.

Appendix 2 - Thoughts on Therapy for ABs as an Identity on the Dissociation Spectrum

The following discussion is intended to assist ABs to find the therapist and the therapy which will meet their needs. It is also intended to inform the treatment options of mental health professionals.

We now understand that being an AB is an identity on the dissociation spectrum. ABs have subjectively real child alters which originated in dissociated childhood trauma. The latter also produces symptoms such as anxiety, depression and eating disorders which can persist through life. It is often a lifetime habit to deny and minimize the impact of distressing feelings and experiences in childhood. It was for me. But if you are AB and you have distress and impairment which seems disproportionate to the objective circumstances of your life, I believe those dysfunctions will not heal without addressing the root cause of childhood trauma. Psychotherapy with a skilled psychotherapist works.

When trauma and a broken childhood attachment are addressed, being an AB can be a healthy personal identity. But when there is distress or impairment, being AB fits with the category of Other Specified Dissociative Disorder (OSDD). That is next door to Dissociative Identity Disorder (DID) on the dissociation spectrum.

This following discusses effective therapy for AB / OSDD. You will be better able to find a suitable therapist if you have some idea of the kind of therapy that you are seeking - and the kind that you are not.

For people with DID, there is already a substantial body of knowledge on effective treatment and therapy, developed by skilled and empathic mental health professionals. (I recommend the books

The Adult Baby – An Identity on the Dissociation Spectrum
by Psychiatrists David Yeung and Colin Ross cited in the references.) There is no similar body of knowledge for ABs.

I reiterate I have no qualifications in psychology. It might be perceived as presumptuous for me to provide any thoughts on therapy. I believe it is justified by the present lack of insight into ABs amongst mental health professionals. I am guided by my own experience of therapy for dissociated trauma and alters some four years ago. I have also drawn on the books of three psychiatrists who understand dissociation and multiples (see their experience cited in Chapter 3). Take what you find useful from this discussion and leave the rest behind.

I am guided by the view of psychiatrist Colin Ross that the treatment for OSDD follows a similar pattern as for DID. He states-

> *"I tell patients that it doesn't really matter where they are on the dissociation spectrum – from no dissociative disorder to full DID – as long as it is clear that they are at least 2/3 or 3/4 of the way out to DID. If that is so, the treatment is pretty much the same, whether they have OSDD or DID. This is important to understand because it interrupts unproductive obsessing about whether the person really has DID or not."*

A similar view is stated by the International Society for the Study of Trauma and Dissociation's (ISSTD) 2010 Guidelines -

> *"In terms of treatment, however, the expert consensus is that DDNOS-1 [the DSM-IV TR label for OSDD] cases—whether they are as-yet-undiagnosed DID or almost-DID—benefit from many of the treatments that have been designed for DID."*

I have quoted extensively from the three psychiatrists. When reading the quotations you may find it helpful to substitute the terms OSDD for DID, and Little or Little(s) for alters.

Diagnosis

As with anyone, the effectiveness of the assistance depends on an accurate diagnosis. That raises a concern. There is a strong prospect being AB will not be understood to be an identity on the dissociation spectrum. In turn, that creates a high risk that a response by a mental health professional will be premised on an inaccurate diagnosis and therefore be ineffective.

The problem starts with the fact dissociation is not well understood by most mental health professionals. The ISSTD's 2010 Guidelines state -

> *"The difficulties in diagnosing DID result primarily from lack of education among clinicians about dissociation, dissociative disorders, and the effects of psychological trauma, as well as from clinician bias. This leads to limited clinical suspicion about dissociative disorders and misconceptions about their clinical presentation."*

This is despite DID or MPD being listed in the DSM since 1980. It is common for people with DID to spend 5 to 10 years being misdiagnosed. Dr Yeung indicates even when he wrote in 2018, many of his colleagues denied DID was real. They preferred other, pathological explanations, and persist in misdiagnosing people with DID.

I suspect a key reason why many mental health professionals don't accept DID is they fear engaging with such a seemingly outlandish condition would diminish their standing as medical scientists. They are afraid of being seen as quacks by skeptical peers or the public.

How much more difficult will it be for ABs to get a valid diagnosis? Firstly, the population of ABs is much smaller than people with DID and hence will be unfamiliar to most therapists. Secondly, being AB is associated in the minds of most mental health professionals with sexual fetishism. That's how it is incorrectly categorized in the DSM, the authoritative catalogue of mental disorders.

This state of affairs is likely to produce -

- a focus on treating the symptoms of dissociation, like depression, anxiety and bulimia, to the exclusion and perhaps to the detriment of the treatment of the primary issue, dissociated trauma; and
- misdiagnoses of distressed or impaired ABs, likely with Borderline Personality Disorder (BPD) or Bi-Polar Affective Disorder or similar.

The problem is that dissociated childhood trauma can produce a complex and confusing array of symptoms. Dr Ross indicates –

"The common comorbid diagnoses in DID include – depression; PTSD; panic disorder; OCD; substance abuse; borderline personality disorder; eating disorders; somatic symptom disorders."

On failing to treat dissociation as the primary issue psychiatrist David Yeung says –

"Treating depression in a DID patient as the primary mood disorder without dealing with the underlying trauma, is like treating a fever with aspirin while ignoring the underlying infection."

He discusses the high probability of misdiagnoses where distress or impairment comes from dissociated trauma-

"In psychiatry, unlike other branches of medicine, diagnosis relies mostly on clinical descriptions, as few laboratory tests are available. In both Bipolar Affective Disorder and Borderline Personality Disorder, for example, one finds abnormal mood changes. When DID is ignored or missed, one of these two diagnoses is invariably dragged in as the explanation for what appears to be cycling between different mood states.

The Adult Baby – An Identity on the Dissociation Spectrum

There is a common misunderstanding which causes this confusion. The switching of affect in in Borderline Personality Disorder (or Bipolar Disorder) is based on the emotional instability of a unitary personality. The apparent switching of affect in MPD [Multiple Personality Disorder / DID] is based on the appearance of different alters. ...

DID often presents as depression and other mood disorders and is commonly misdiagnosed as Borderline Personality Disorder, Bipolar Disorder and Treatment Resistant Depression. If the clinician is not wary, it can be confused with Schizophrenia as well. These misdiagnoses are based on an inappropriately low level of suspicion for DID. The confusion is compounded by exclusively biological view of mental illness and the unfortunate over-reliance on pharmacological approaches to treatment. The resulting ongoing, under-reporting of DID leads to a misperception that DID is extremely rare."

"The misdiagnoses of DID patients are the result of misunderstanding the etiology of changing emotional presentations. There are four basic target symptoms in psycho-pharmacology: mood fluctuation, psychosis, anxiety, and depression. Psychiatrists who are trained to look primarily for these target symptoms will seize the symptom(s) and prescribe medication accordingly, rather than look deeper into the roots of the symptomology." [Engaging Multiple Personalities Volume 2]

If the mental health professional is not sufficiently knowledgeable or skilled, dissociated childhood trauma will not be diagnosed. It will continue to drive symptoms of distress or impairment which are then labelled as treatment-resistant.

It takes a skilled mental health professional to see beyond individual symptoms and recognize the underlying cause common to each of them. Dr Ross describes the perspective required -

The Adult Baby – An Identity on the Dissociation Spectrum

"Another motto of Trauma Model Therapy is the problem is not the problem. This means that the presenting symptom, behavior, addiction, social role, or diagnosis is not the problem: it is the solution to a problem in the background. This doesn't mean that the problem is not a problem, or can be ignored. It means that the symptom or behavior occurs in a context, has a meaning and function, is a survival strategy, and can best be understood in the context of the person's life story. The symptom is not just the brain on the fritz or a symptom of neurotransmitter imbalance.

The therapist's job is to figure out the function or purpose of the behavior and the problem in the background it is meant to solve. The treatment goal is then to help the person find a better way to solve the problem in the background, so she can let go of the unhealthy coping strategy."

The categorization of being AB as a sexual fetish in the DSM is an example of the failure described above – mistaking a symptom for the cause of the condition.

To be fair, ABs have probably contributed to some of the dismal history of their reception by mental health professionals. I suspect many ABs seeking treatment for symptoms such as anxiety, depression or bulimia do not realize this has any relationship to their being AB (ie. comes from the same source). Or they have an undefined fear it does but are too scared of being harshly judged to disclose being AB. I suspect it is rare for ABs to disclose the full extent of the tormenting conflicts of the 'binge and purge' cycle; the involuntary triggering; or the extent of the identification in their fantasies with being a helpless, dependent baby. The fear behind this non-disclosure is perfectly valid. Most mental health professionals have no understanding of ABs and many would quickly label these symptoms as a pathological psycho-sexual disorder as per the DSM. But it's a vicious cycle. Without this knowledge, there are no indications which might point the more insightful therapists to the real origin of being AB in dissociated childhood trauma.

The Adult Baby – An Identity on the Dissociation Spectrum

Over time, things will get better. The awareness of dissociation is growing, albeit from a low base. Chapter 3 cited studies which suggest around 10 per cent of the population has substantial symptoms of dissociation. That makes dissociation as prevalent as mood disorders such as depression and anxiety. It took decades, but awareness of these mood disorders has grown amongst the public and mental health professionals. That has reduced their stigma and increased the prospect of receiving appropriate treatment. In time it is likely the awareness of dissociation will follow the same trajectory.

That's not much help right now.

Finding a Therapist

The current situation places an onus on ABs, and those who love them, to insist on an accurate diagnosis and appropriate treatment, and to find a mental health professional capable of providing both. Treating dissociation is a specialist branch of psychotherapy. (For guidance on selecting a mental health professional see the appendix in my book 'The Adult Baby Identity – A Self Help Guide').

An AB needs to find a therapist who –

- accepts the existence of subjectively real alters created in childhood trauma (as per the DSM), AND
- believes in an outcome where alters and the host work as a team or family, rather than requiring the alters to fuse with the host to create a unitary psyche (as discussed in Chapter 14).

The first point needs a therapist who can see beyond the nappies et al to the dissociated child alters and trauma behind it. It's good if they have some experience with treating dissociation, but even if they don't but are willing to learn it's a good start. The mental health professionals who successfully treated Christine Pattillo and Robert Oxnam didn't have a lot of experience with DID when they first started treating Christine and Robert.

The second point needs a therapist who adheres to humanistic psychology that respects the self-determination of the client, rather than believing they know better what is good for the client.

So the therapist you are looking for is likely to combine an unusual level of empathy, an open mind and professional courage.

What to Look For In Treatment/Therapy

I believe if you an AB / OSDD the most effective therapy would reflect the following: –

1. psychotherapy is likely to be more helpful than medication or hypnosis;
2. effective psychotherapy for multiples is based on working with alters;
3. psychotherapy does not require reliving the original trauma;
4. much of the healing is self-directed;
5. the support of loved ones, especially a loving partner, is invaluable;
6. if you have a consoling faith, don't be afraid to draw on it;
7. you define what the end goal of therapy means for you; and
8. it's okay to provisionally self-diagnose to provide a starting point for therapy.

Each of these is discussed below.

Psychotherapy is Likely to be More Useful Than Medication or Hypnosis

Several of the psychiatrists cited in the book indicate dissociation generally does not respond to drug treatment. Medication may be used to address symptoms such as depression, anxiety or sleep disturbances to allow an interval for the treatment of the underlying cause, dissociated trauma. But medication is unlikely to heal the causes of those symptoms.

Psychiatrist Dr Colin Ross says –

"In some cases, medications can be very helpful in managing some presenting symptoms (eg. depression, insomnia). Some medications may have small positive impacts on certain post-traumatic symptoms. However, until now, there is no evidence that medications can help a person process and integrate his/her trauma or dissociated parts of the personality. It is also important to be aware of the potential side effects of medications. In the literature, it has been reported that some medications may worsen certain dissociative symptoms. Different dissociated personality states of the same person may respond to medications differently. Psychosocial interventions (eg. psychotherapy) are primary treatments for post traumatic mental disorders." [Be a Teammate With Yourself: Understanding Trauma and Dissociation]

The appropriate treatment for dissociated childhood trauma is psychotherapy – 'the talking cure'. The good news is with an accurate diagnosis, psychotherapy is effective. For example, the greater majority of people with DID who receive psychotherapy have positive life outcomes.

Dr Ross says–

"The main conclusion [of studies], though, is that the psychotherapy of dissociative disorders is evidence-based and effective."

Hypnosis has value only as an ancillary to psychotherapy. Careful therapists like Dr Steinberg see a role for hypnosis in relaxation techniques and the like. However, the use of hypnosis to 'call out' secretive or reluctant alters, or to elicit memories of childhood abuse is dangerous and potentially harmful. Therapists who use these practices should be avoided.

The Adult Baby – An Identity on the Dissociation Spectrum

In the 1990s, in the first stage of treating DID at least one leading authority (Richard Kluft) promoted the use of hypnosis as central to treatment. In more recent times both psychiatrists David Yeung and Jeffrey Smith did not favour hypnosis. Jeffrey Smith states –

> *"... hypnosis seemed controlling and manipulative, and multiples have already had enough of this type of experience for a lifetime. It seemed to place the doctor too much in charge. My experience of treatment is much more as a partnership in which the patient brings knowledge about his or her inner life and I contribute my understanding of people and my personal reactions. Together, we pool our information and work on healing."*

Effective Psychotherapy for Multiplies is Based on Working with Alters

The central fact about being a 'multiple' is you have subjectively real alters. Recognizing and accepting this, for both you and your therapist, is the key to effective psychotherapy. The three psychiatrists agree on that.

Don't be afraid of your alters. They may have scared you at times with their unexpected power to influence your thoughts, feelings and actions. But you have the power to heal and change wounded or dysfunctional alters. Finding out you have a subjectively real child alter doesn't mean you have to hand your whole life and psyche over to them. Nor does it mean your partner or your therapist have to acquiesce to all the demands of a hurt and angry alter. You can learn to live together happily, without disruption or dysfunction. In therapy and healing, you and your therapist respond compassionately but firmly to a demanding or dysfunctional child alter just as you would to a distressed and angry small biological child.

Psychiatrist Dr David Yeung says –

The Adult Baby – An Identity on the Dissociation Spectrum

"The heart of DID therapy is engaging alters on their own terms."

"Treating a person with DID means developing an attitude of compassion and respect towards the alters whenever and however they emerge, whether it be shyly, boldly, flirtatiously or aggressively. Successful treatment of the alters does not mean eradication of them or their functions."

"Common courtesy – and the necessity of establishing a therapeutic bond – dictates that a therapist speak to each alter as if he or she is an individual. This requires a willingness on the part of the therapist to engage the dissociation in therapy. Many therapists may be unable to do this for personal or philosophical reasons.

Therapists may be stuck in the paradigm that alters are pathological manifestations and therefore they should neither be acknowledged for spoken to. In treating patients with schizophrenic hallucinations, psychiatrists try to persuade them to ignore the voices that they hear. In DID therapy, to the contrary, communication between the therapist and an alter, as well as among alters, is fundamental to successful therapy."

... a key principle of MPD treatment; to treat each single MPD patient as if I was conducting group therapy. Knowing they [the alters] are all listening, one can start talking to them as a group."

The ISSTD's 2010 Guidelines state -

"Helping the identities to be aware of one another as legitimate parts of the self and to negotiate and resolve their conflicts is at the very core of the therapeutic process. It is countertherapeutic for the therapist to treat any alternate identity as if it were more "real" or more important than any other. The therapist should not "play favorites" among the alternate identities or exclude apparently unlikable or disruptive ones from the therapy ... The therapist should foster

the idea that all alternate identities represent adaptive attempts to cope or to master problems that the patient has faced. Thus, it is countertherapeutic to tell patients to ignore or "get rid" of identities … "

I have had successful therapy which recognized and worked with my child alters. If you are self-conscious and inhibited like I am, you do not have to speak as an alter. Dr Ross says-

"Talking through means that you talk to an alter in the background while another part – usually the host – is in executive control. The part then answers inside the person's head and the host passes on that by saying it out loud. Not uncommonly, after a few questions and answers, the alter emerges spontaneously. If this happens, I acknowledge the switch, confirm who I'm talking to, and carry on with the conversation. …"

Effective psychotherapy does not require a detailed biography of every alter. Dr Yeung advises mental health professionals –

"As a general rule, resist the temptation to try and find out more about these alters. Once their function is clear – such as holding an emotional aspect of a traumatic experience – that is all that is needed for therapy. Knowing their function enables the therapist to acknowledge and work with whatever the alter is holding. This is a far more important task than exploring the personality specifics, the storyline, of each individual alter." [Engaging Multiple Personalities Volume 2]

Dr Yeung's comments point to the difference in perspective between a mental health professional treating distress and impairment, and a person who sees being a 'multiple' as their personal identity. It isn't necessary for a therapist to know the 'life story' of each alter to provide effective therapy. But for ABs, I believe it is psychologically healthy to get to know your alter(s). But that is part of the normal process of human growth and discovery which everyone does for themselves.

The Adult Baby – An Identity on the Dissociation Spectrum

Colin Ross emphasizes in working with alters, neither the AB, nor the therapist can lose sight of the 'whole person' -

> "Treat the person who has the DID, not the DID. This will involve working with the DID, but while you're working with the parts, keep a firm grip on the whole person perspective. This is a single person with human problems that are fragmented into parts. You have to work with the parts to help the single parts; but there is only one person there ..."

Healing trauma and building cooperation with alters are the two key objectives of therapy for 'multiples'. Dr Smith says –

> "... there are just two therapeutic goals. The first is to process and detoxify the buried memories of trauma and the second is to help the long-separated parts come to know, respect, and ultimately love one another. As these are accomplished, continuing to remain a multiple will no longer be a necessity but a choice."

All the psychiatrists accept these two objectives. But there can be differences between them in terms of which is more important. Dr Yeung emphasizes the primary importance of healing trauma whereas Dr Colin Ross emphasizes the healthy functioning of alters. Dr Ross says -

> "In any case, trauma memories are only one topic in DID therapy – I don't think they are the main one. A lot of the work involves learning grounding and self-soothing skills, and self-regulation, saying 'no' to addictions, correcting cognitive errors, forming healthy relationships and other tasks that aren't 'memory work' as such. In DID, additional tasks include: orienting alters to the body and the present; building inter-personality communication and cooperation – building a team; building co-consciousness and co-presence; reducing host resistance; and other tasks which are not directly connected to memories as such."

Psychotherapy Does Not Require Re-living the Original Trauma

I suspect a key reason for denying or minimizing distressing experiences in childhood is we fear 'touching that hotplate again' – reliving something very painful. Effective psychotherapy does <u>not</u> require people with dissociated trauma remember and relive every frightening detail.

Contemporary treatment of dissociated trauma emphasizes several purposes –

1. to initially stablise a person by allowing them to recognize the distressing sensations belong to past events and they are safe in the present; and
2. subsequently, to build a 'trauma narrative' which allows the person sufficient understanding of what happened to make sense of their response.

Of the first point, Dr Yeung says –

"Patients must learn to know when they are ready to venture inward and explore more deeply. They need to be taught and actually experience the key fact that processing the trauma in order to gain some sense of mastery over it is <u>not</u> the same as reliving it. It is also not the same as just talking about it. It is about touching the wound lightly, experiencing and recognizing the discrepancy between one's heightened arousal and the actual situation happening right now in a safe place, where there is no threat."

The memory of trauma has a special character. People can accurately recall the subjective sensations caused by trauma – the emotions, thoughts and physical sensations. The memory of objective detail – where, when, who – can be more difficult and unreliable. There are well-understood reasons for these differences in recall in terms of how the brain functions (see the discussion in Chapter 3). The point is, the validity of a person's recall of their subjective experience does not depend on forensically accurate recall of objective details. Creating a trauma narrative is about reconstructing a sufficient understanding of what happened long ago to make sense of it, without needing it to satisfy some forensic or legal requirement.

Dr Smith helpfully distinguishes the two healing mechanisms at work in the therapeutic recall of past trauma.

> *"The first is the mechanism by which painful experiences are detoxified. ... I will refer to this by its original name catharsis. The second is the process by which negative values, attitudes, and attachments derived from abusers are modified. I will refer to this healing mechanism as internalization. Both mechanisms may be involved in any phase of therapeutic work.*
>
> *It is important to note that internalization works differently with multiples than it does with others. What is internalized belongs to one alter, not to the whole. ... Some alters become the embodiments of destructive and self-negating attitudes so that others can be spared. This naturally leads to tensions among alters, rather than ambivalence within oneself, as is the case with other trauma survivors. In fact, it is the healing of these tensions that constitutes the major therapeutic goal along with the healing of painful experiences. Thus, internalization is the key therapeutic goal of bringing alters together, while catharsis is the process most closely allied to working with traumatic memories."*

The internalization of negative messages can happen in other forms of trauma than abuse. The experience of not being protected or able to turn to a parent figure for help, can make a child feel unloved and unloveable. And as with abuse, instead of laying that feeling with an adult on whom they are dependent, the child's unconscious invents reasons why they were unloveable.

Most of the Healing is Self-Directed

Based on the published material it is common for people with DID to be in therapy for many years. This lengthy treatment was due to the depth and harm of the childhood abuse, and the strength of the denial of being a multiple.

If the estimates people with DID represent one per cent of the population are valid, then the published accounts may not be representative. For every person who can find and afford a therapist to be in treatment for many years, there must be many others who have to, or chose to, take a different road. There simply aren't the number of skilled therapists around to treat everyone for that length of time.

The numbers suggest there must be many people with substantial dissociative symptoms who have more positive outcomes but who have to rely more on their own psychological resources. There is a pointer towards this even in the published cases of lengthy treatment. Two of the psychiatrists emphasize even in those latter contexts much of the healing is self-directed.

Dr Smith says –

"Multiples seem to have their own blueprint for healing, and one of the main contributions a therapist can make is to recognize and value the patient's inner direction."

Dr Yeung says –

"I firmly believe that all therapy contains a large measure of self healing. DID patients need to develop the confidence to take up a measure of self-directed therapy. It is necessary for the alters to cooperate and work as a team. The therapist must encourage the patient's to do this."

I suspect for most people who are AB / OSDD the level of childhood trauma is less than for people with DID. This makes it both possible, and likely, their healing will be largely self-directed and will not require the kind of lengthy therapy found in published accounts of people with DID. In my case, the therapy took months rather than years.

Much of this healing will be concerned less with trauma, and more with the broken bond in childhood with the AB's mother/primary caregiver. The latter is called an insecure attachment (see Chapter 11) and is common amongst the broader population. See Jasmin Lee Cori's excellent book *'The Emotionally Absent Mother: How to Recognize and Heal the Invisible Effects of Childhood Emotional Neglect'* for self-directed healing of an insecure childhood attachment.

Support of A Loving Partner

I believe over the long run, the most important sources of healing for someone with AB / OSDD are themselves, the support of a loving partner, and the assistance of a skilled therapist, in that order.

In the healing process, the acceptance of a partner relieves someone with AB / OSDD of the burden of having to fight denial by themselves. In everyday life, the acceptance of a partner means we are not alone with our doubt and cognitive dissonance.

Dr Yeung gives the inspiring example in his casebook of 'Joan' whose husband was an indispensable partner in his wife's healing and full recovery from fragmented DID (*'Engaging Multiple Personalities Volume 1'* Chapter 1). Joan's husband's level of participation in her therapy was unusual, but it is a pointer to the obvious fact your partner is a far more constant and significant presence in your life than any therapist, and their empathy is powerful. That is affirmed in Christine Pattillo's account of her husband Christopher's support through her diagnosis and treatment, and Cameron West's account of his wife Rikki's support.

Consoling Faith

If you have a consoling faith in God or a higher power, don't be afraid to call on it. Dr Yeung, who treated around one hundred people with DID over his career, welcomed such faith and saw it as a source of resilience. In his book *'Engaging Multiple Personalities Volume 1'* (Chapter 5) he gives a case history for 'Ruth', a young woman who persistently pursued successful healing in the face of great obstacles, because of the strength she drew from her faith.

If you are a multiple, your dissociation and alters are not beyond your faith. God loves all of you, including your alters. The therapist I saw about my childhood trauma and my alters worked with my faith in the therapy. I found that made therapy easier and more effective.

You Define the End Goal of Therapy

There are two expert views about the intended outcome of therapy for multiples (as discussed in Chapter 14). One is to fuse alters with the host to create a unitary psyche – in essence, to stop being a multiple. The other is to continue being a multiple and for the alters to work as a cooperative team or family.

Those who favour fusion see it in the following terms. The alters merge with the host and the positive capabilities and traits of the alters are not lost but become available to the whole psyche. The damage and the pain originally held by the alters from the original trauma(s) is resolved in therapy before fusion and is not carried forward. The person now has a unitary psyche. There are no 'fault lines' remaining in the psyche which might again fracture in the face of future stresses or crises. To effect fusion requires years of intensive weekly therapy.

Those who favour cooperation see it in the following terms. The alters are like a family, each loving and respecting the others and their different roles within the psyche. There is no amnesia and all the alters are co-conscious. Shifting is more common than switching. The alters may be co-present.

The key point is, it's your choice about which outcome you want. You need to find a therapist who respects your self-determination and doesn't have a hidden agenda to push you towards their favoured option.

The Adult Baby – An Identity on the Dissociation Spectrum
Provisional Self Diagnosis is Okay

After researching this book one of the questions I had for myself was what do I do if I need to seek therapy again in the future? Do I declare to a psychotherapist what I now understand about ABs being on the dissociation spectrum? My concern is they will be dis-believing and pissed off I am usurping their professional skills to make a diagnosis. It's tough enough talking about being AB without making the initial interview any harder. And we live in the age of Dr Google and Dr Wikipedia which I am sure pisses off many mental health professionals.

I was comforted to read the following from psychiatrist Colin Ross, an authority on dissociation -

> *"A person with DID that hasn't yet been officially diagnosed may or may not already know they have DID. Some people have done reading and research, are aware of having blank spells, know some of their parts by name and age, and really only need confirmation of the diagnosis."*

So, if I do seek therapy in the future, I will declare what I understand about my AB identity. To do otherwise would seem like wasting time and money in dancing around the bushes. My understanding of myself is going to have to be 'on the table' sooner or later. I will try and hold my views lightly and respect that a skilled psychotherapist is going to bring knowledge and insights 'to the table' that I don't have. Effective therapy is a collaboration between the client and the therapist. It works best when each respects what the other brings to the collaboration.

Glossary

The book uses the following terms.

See also the discussion at the beginning of Chapter 4 on terminology relevant to DID and 'multiples'.

AB	Adult Baby – adolescents or adults or wear diapers/nappies and are attracted to the trappings and

	fantasy of infancy
alter	alternative personality
B&D	bondage and discipline
cognitive dissonance	the mental discomfort (psychological stress) experienced by a person who holds two or more contradictory beliefs, ideas, or values
DDNOS	Dissociative Disorder Not Otherwise Specified – the category below DID on the dissociation spectrum – introduced in the DSM-IV TR, the penultimate version of the DSM
DID	Dissociative Identity Disorder – previously known as Multiple Personality Disorder (MPD)
differential diagnosis	A systematic diagnostic method used to identify a condition where multiple alternatives are possible. It is akin to the process of elimination and involves matching symptoms with the attributes of alternative conditions to find which condition best explains all the symptoms.
DL	Diaper Lover – adolescents or adults who wear diapers/nappies but do not acknowledge any other attraction to the trappings of infancy
DSM	Diagnostic and Statistical Manual of Mental Disorders - the standard diagnostic tool published by the American Psychiatric Association. The latest version,

	the DSM-5 was published in 2013. The DSM is one of two classification systems for mental disorders. The other is the ICD (International Classification of Diseases)-10 Classification of Mental and Behavioural Disorders, produced by the World Health Organization. The DSM is generally used in the US (and Australia?), while the ICD is used more widely in Europe and other parts of the world. For a discussion of the treatment of dissociative disorders in the DSM and ICD, see Rob Spring's blog 'DSM-5: what's new in the criteria for dissociative disorders?' (cited in the references).
fetish	The clinical term for fetish is a paraphilia. The penultimate version of the DSM, the DSM-IV-TR, describes paraphilias as "recurrent, intense sexually arousing fantasies, sexual urges or behaviors generally involving nonhuman objects, the suffering or humiliation of oneself or one's partner, or children or other nonconsenting persons that occur over a period of six months." It includes fetishism (which covers ABs), exhibitionism (flashing), frotteurism (groping), pedophilia (child molesting), voyeurism (peeping toms), and transvestism (cross dressing). The inclusion of consenting and non-consenting (coercive, illegal) behaviours under the same definition is unhelpful and unnecessarily stigmatizing (for the former).
host	the alternative personality who is out in front most of the time
ISSTD	International Society for the Study of Trauma and Dissociation
Little	The term AB's often use for the child part of their

	psyche. For the purposes of this book it is construed as referring to a child alter.
mental health professionals	Psychiatrists, psychologists, therapists and counsellors
MPD	Multiple Personality Disorder – the old term for Dissociative Identity Disorder
multiple	A person with alternative personalities
OSDD	Other Specified Dissociative Disorder – the category below DID on the dissociation spectrum - replaces DDNOS in the DSM-5, the latest version of the DSM
singleton	A person with no alternative personalities
trigger	A sensory input (sight, sound, smell etc) that causes a change (switch) in the alter which is in executive control of a multiple's body.

Annotated List of References
Books on DID and Dissociation

There is a vast literature on dissociation and Dissociative Identity Disorder (DID), including autobiographies of people with DID, and material by mental health professionals. A search on Amazon will produce a large selection. I chose amongst the material that was accessible and affordable and seemed insightful in the case of autobiographies, and authoritative in the case of the non-fiction material.

There is a good reading list of authors with DID, writing about DID at –

http://www.zoramquynh.com/a-did-book-list/

Ehling, T; Nijenhius, E.R.S.; Krikke, A.P	'Volume of discrete brain structures in complex dissociative disorders: preliminary findings' in Progress in Brain Research, Vol. 167, 2008, E.R. de Kloet, M.S. Oitzl & E. Vermetten (Eds.)
	Succinct and readily comprehensible to the lay reader. Useful list of references.
	Available free on-line at –
	https://s3.amazonaws.com/academia.edu.documents/45354174/Volume_of_discrete_brain_structures_in_c20160504-793-1b98uyu.pdf?response-content
International Society for the Study of Trauma and Dissociation	Guidelines for Treating Dissociative Identity Disorder in Adults, Third Revision
	Succinct and useful. Imbued with the adverse, 'fusionist' view of alters. Includes abreaction &

	hypnosis in treatment options. Has a comprehensive list of authoritative references as at 2010. Can be accessed at – https://www.isst-d.org/wp-content/uploads/2019/02/GUIDELINES_REVISED2011.pdf
Kate, Mary-Anne, Jamieson, Graham & Hopgood, Tanya	The prevalence of Dissociative Disorders and dissociative experiences in college populations: a meta-analysis of 98 studies. Journal of Trauma & Dissociation Can be accessed at - https://www.researchgate.net/profile/Mary_Anne_Kate A statistical meta-analysis (a study of studies) testing whether dissociative disorders are linked to trauma or suggestable fantasy. The article affirms the former and finds an incidence across countries of dissociative disorders of the magnitude of 10% of the population. Dry and technical.
Oxnam, Robert B.	A Fractured Mind: My Life With Multiple Personality Disorder (2013) (digital and hardcopy: Amazon). The author was a prominent US academic. Shows his treatment journey from the inside. Includes an insightful essay on the nature and treatment of DID by the author's psychiatrist Jeffrey Smith.
Pattillo, Christine, and the Gang	I Am We: Living With Multiple Personalities (2014) (digital and hardcopy: Amazon) This remarkable account has the voice of the host,

	each alter, and the host's husband and mother. She lives openly as a 'multiple' and her husband embraces her alters as his family. Shows compelling courage and warmth. Highly recommended. Digitial copies are inexpensive. Search on 'Christine Pattillo' for her clips on YouTube
Ross, Colin A.	Treatment of Dissociative Identity Disorder: Techniques and Strategies for Stabilisation (2018) (digital and hardcopy: Amazon) A practical, pragmatic and concise guide to life with alters. The author is an authority on trauma and dissociation and has written a key textbook on DID. Highly recommended.
	Dissociative Identity Disorder: Diagnosis, Clinical Features, and Treatment of Multiple Personality. Second Edition (1997). Available in hardcopy only, second hand only (try abebooks) An update of the original 1989 text on DID. Authoritative in its comprehensive scope and detail. The author's views can be respected without agreeing with them.
Ross, Colin A.	Be A Teammate With Yourself: Understanding Trauma and Dissociation (2019) (digital and hardcopy: Amazon) Useful coverage of the topics. I prefer the author's other recent work 'Treatment of Dissociative Identity

	Disorder'.
Spring, Rob	'DSM-5: what's new in the criteria for dissociative disorders?' PODS (Positive Outcomes for Dissociative Survivors) Website. Posted 9 January 2013 A useful description of the treatment of dissociative disorders in the latest version of the DSM. Can be accessed at - https://information.pods-online.org.uk/dsm-5-whats-new-in-the-criteria-for-dissociative-disorders/
	'DID or DDNOS: does it matter?' PODS (Positive Outcomes for Dissociative Survivors) Website. Posted 1 May 2013 An insightful article exploring the sub-DID part of the dissociation spectrum. Highly recommended. Can be accessed at - https://information.pods-online.org.uk/did-or-ddnos-does-it-matter/
Steele, Kathy; Boon, Suzette; van der Hart, Onno.	Treating Trauma Related Dissociation: A Practical Integrative Approach. (2016) (digital and hard copy: Amazon). A text for therapists. Notable for its pejorative treatment of alters. Promotes manipulative, ethically

	doubtful intransigence by therapists working with DID clients. The approach appears to have been inappropriately transferred from DBT therapy with PTSD & BPD. Expensive. Not recommended.
Steinberg, Marlene	The Stranger in the Mirror: Dissociation The Hidden Epidemic (2010) (hardcopy: Harper Collins. Digital: Amazon). Excellent at explaining dissociation. The author is the psychiatrist who developed the leading diagnostic questionnaire for identifying dissociative disorders. Highly recommended.
Trujillo, Olga	The Sum of My Parts: A Survivor's Story of Dissociative Identity Disorder (2011) (digital & paperback: Amazon) A story of great courage surviving severe abuse. The first half is concerned with the abuse (v. confronting), and the second with treatment based on the first-generation understanding of DID. The author was a high powered Justice Department lawyer.
Vermetten, Eric; Schmahl, Christian; Lindner, Sanneke; Loewenstein, Richard J; Bremner, Douglas J	'Hippocampal and Amygdalar Volumes in Dissociative Identity Disorder' American Journal of Psychiatry. 2006 Apr; 163(4): 630–636. Succinct and readily comprehensible to the lay reader. Claims to be the first study to demonstrate different brain structures in DID. Useful list of

	references. Available free on-line at – https://www.ncbi.nlm.nih.gov/pmc/articles/PMC32 33754/
W, A.T.	Got Parts: An Insider's Guide to Managing Life Successfully with Dissociative Identity Disorder. (2005) (digital & paperback: amazon) A good self help book, recommended to me by a family member with DID (Dax). It is relevant to anyone with multiplicity of consciousness. Digital copies are inexpensive.
Walker, Herschel	Breaking Free: My Life with Dissociative Identity Disorder. (2008) (Digital: Amazon. Hardcopy: Touchstone) The author is a highly successful NFL player. His DID did not originate with sexual abuse but principally from prolonged bullying.
West, Cameron	First Person Plural: My Life As a Multiple (2013 edition) (Digital: Amazon) Has powerful insights into denial, treatment, & DID in a loving marriage. He and his wife embraced his alters. Highly recommended.
Wikipedia	Amygdala

	Dissociation (psychology)
	Dissociative Disorder Not Otherwise Specified
	Dissociative Identity Disorder *
	Herschel Walker
	Hippocampus
	* The article on DID has some useful material. However it conveys a misleading view of the validity of DID. It gives equal credence to the view DID is the product of fantasy/false memory. This is false equivalence. It is the same as an article on the Earth giving equal credence to the 'flat earth theory', and on this basis declaring the Earth being round is a 'controversial' theory.
Yeung, David	Engaging Multiple Personalities (Volume 1): Contextual Case Histories (2018) (Digitial & hardcopy: Amazon). 14 case histories of people with DID from the practice of a retired psychiatrist. Shows the unique character of each, and differing outcomes. Compelling and insightful. Highly recommended. Digital copies are inexpensive.
	Engaging Multiple Personalities (Volume 2): Therapeutic Guidelines (2018) (Digitial & hardcopy: Amazon) Intended to guide and encourage other mental health professionals to treat people with DID. Consolidates the insights from Volume 1. I prefer the latter as the case histories are notably insightful.

	Engaging Multiple Personalities (Volume 3): Living in Multiplicity (2018) (Digital: Amazon). A guide for people with DID written by a retired psychiatrist who had many DID clients. Written as a question-and-answer format between the author and an imagined recently diagnosed client with DID. Repetitive but insightful.

Books on ABs and Other Topics

By contrast to DID the non-fiction literature on adult babies is sparse. That includes life histories/autobiographies, self help material, and empathic and insightful material by mental health professionals. Most of this is cited in the annotated references to my book *'The Adult Baby Identity – Coming Out As An Adult Baby',* and most of it is published by abdiscovery.com.au and available from there or Amazon.

Bader, Michael	Arousal: The Secret Logic of Sexual Fantasies (2003) (Virgin Books) (ISBN 0 7535 0739 0) Paperback only. No digital copy. Highly recommended for anyone wanting to understand troubling sexual fantasies. Finds the emotional meaning of fantasies with compassion and insight. The author is a gifted intuitive psychotherapist.
Bent, Michael	Being an Adult Baby: Articles and Essays on Being an Adult Baby. (2016) (Amazon & Abdiscovery.com.au)

	A collection of insightful and thought provoking articles on the AB identity. Notably – 'Identity Confusion in the Adult Baby', 'Finding Balance Between the Baby and the Adult', and 'Binge and Purge'.'
Bent, Rosalie	There's Still A Baby in My Bed: Learning To Live Happily With the Adult Baby in Your Relationship. (2015) (Amazon & Abdiscovery.com.au) A revised version of the ground breaking 2012 book that first articulated being an AB was a personal identity, not just a fetish. Written by the wife of an AB. Evergreen.
	'When it all goes wrong' Rosalie Bent's on-line blog entry for 26 March 2013 See – https://rosaliebent.wordpress.com/
Conrad, Felix	Transgender: Fact or Fetish (2016) (Digital: Amazon) Takes issue with sexologists view of transgender as a fetish. There is a parallel between this and AB's issue with their identity being similarly categorized. Insightful. Includes the insight the target of erotic fantasies may not be sex with a partner, but transformation of the self to the desired form (the desired gender for transgender people). Recommended.

	See Conrad's blogs at – https://novagirl.net/latest-articles-2
	How to Jedi Mind Trick Your Gender Dysphoria (2016) (Digital: Amazon) The intended audience are people who identify as transgender but decided not to transition. Iconoclastic and insightful.
	Quantum Desire: A Sexological Analysis of Crossdreaming (2016) (Digital: Amazon) Makes the case for an inclusive definition of transgender which includes those who identify as crossdressers or with a sissy fetish. There is a parallel between the author's view of the transgender identity and my view of the AB identity.
Cori, Jasmin Lee	The Emotionally Absent Mother: How to Recognize and Heal the Invisible Effects of Childhood Emotional Neglect (Second Edition) (2017) (digital & paperback: Amazon) A brilliantly written discussion of insecure attachments in childhood and their effects. Makes Attachment Theory, Bowlby and Winnicott accessible to the lay reader. Highly recommended and inexpensive.
Joyce, Maggie	The Full Time Permanent Adult Infant (2019) (Amazon & Abdiscovery.com.au)

	An account of an AB living a 24/7 AB lifestyle by their wife, and the mother of their 'Little'. I disagree with the author on key points, but it is a work of courageous honesty.
Lewis, Dylan	The Adult Baby Identity – Healing Childhood Wounds (2019) (Amazon & Abdiscovery.com.au) Explores the origins of the identity in an insecure attachment and trauma in childhood. References John Bowlby and Attachment Theory, and Donald Winnicott.
	The Adult Baby Identity – A Self Help Guide (2019) (Amazon & Abdiscovery.com.au) Focuses on self acceptance and resolving the internal conflict between the Inner Child, Inner Parent and Adult.
	The Adult Baby Identity – Coming Out as an Adult Baby (2019) (Amazon & Abdiscovery.com.au) Makes the case being AB is a minority personal identity and considers the stages by which the identity is formed.
	Living With Chrissie: My Life As An Adult Baby (2018) (Amazon & Abdiscovery.com.au My account of my life as a very late bloomer as an AB

	('better late than never').
Wikipedia	Cognitive dissonance Regression (psychology)
Winnicott, Donald W.	'Transitional Objects and Transitional Phenomena—A Study of the First Not-Me Possession' (1953) International Journal of Psycho-Analysis, 34:89-97 Winnicott's ground breaking original exposition on the subject. Includes concise statement of Winnicott's view of infant psychological development. Available free, on-line at – https://pdfs.semanticscholar.org/a56f/ba056a2103 9574e5b2371f4ad01728b54366.pdf
	'Playing and Reality' (1971) Tavistock Publications. (hardcopy only, no digital copy) Recommended for those with a keen interest in Winnicott. Written for psychotherapists. Best read after reading some secondary sources, or Winnicott's books for laypeople. A seminal book published in the last year of Winnicott's life.

CPSIA information can be obtained
at www.ICGtesting.com
Printed in the USA
LVHW041323071019
633401LV00004B/532/P

9 781694 645807